CHRIS

THE BASKETBALL
PATH

A PRACTICAL GUIDE TO THE **MENTAL GAME**, **DISCIPLINE**, AND **PERSONAL GROWTH** FOR BALLPLAYERS

First edition 2022

www.strideyourpassion.com

StrideYourPassion Sàrl

Paperback: 978-2-9701612-9-5
Ebook file: 978-2-9701612-8-8

Table of Contents

Dedication

"Basketball isn't about the bright lights, packed arenas, and highlight reels. Basketball is a way of life. Basketball is a relationship between you and the ball, you and your teammates. If you love the game, nobody can take that away from you."

—Michael Jordan

To all the players who are passionate about the game and are in the quest of finding ways to improve. For anyone involved in the game, from the ones discovering it to the elite competitors. To those pushing to make a career out of basketball, and those who are simply trying to improve and enjoy the grind of becoming a better player day after day. This book is for you.

Basketball is beautiful. Embrace it.

***Please note that for simplicity's sake, the term "player", abbreviated with the masculine pronouns him, his, and himself were used throughout the book to designate any player, both masculine, feminine, and those not associating with a gender.**

Expressing both masculine and feminine pronouns each time (as I initially did) proved to be annoying for the lector, and using non-genre pronouns added difficulty and confusion to the writing process.

The same approach was used when talking about team coaches.

THE BASKETBALL PATH

An Improbable Coincidence

2 a.m., March 19, 2007
Geneva, Switzerland

I was sitting in front of the TV, in my hometown of Versoix, Switzerland (near Geneva). On the screen, the magic of the NCAA March Madness[1] played out. Two of college basketball's most storied programs, the Kansas Jayhawks and the Kentucky Wildcats, squared off in the second round of the NCAA Tournament.

For the first time in my life, I was able to see a March Madness game.

With today's availability of social media and streaming, it is hard to grasp. But in those days, the NCAA and its national tournament, March Madness, was still relatively unknown in my home country of Switzerland. Even some basketball players didn't know about it, and very few people had access

---

[1] NCAA March Madness: Each year, the National Collegiate Athletic Association (NCAA) holds its national championship tournament during the month of March. With 68 teams battling in a single-elimination event, and all the passion and drama these games whip up, the tournament is known as March Madness.

to the rare channels broadcasting the games. On top of the struggle of staying up late into the night to watch these games, it was an even tougher challenge to know who had access to those TV channels.

My teammate Paul and I were sitting together, watching those physical monsters compete. We stared at the TV as though the game was being broadcast from a different planet, from an inaccessible place, where basketball was all people cared about. A place resembling a glorious dream. I watched with fierce attention, scrutinizing every player, every move, every shot in an attempt to spot what made these players special and to gain something to implement in my game.

At some point, the camera zoomed in on the Kansas bench. Down the line, I witnessed the players, their broad shoulders and arms sculpted like Greek statues. At this moment, I was awestruck. *Those guys are not made out of the same stuff I am made of,* I thought.

I watched this in silence as my heart sank, my aspirations to play one day in the NCAA being crushed. *That place is reserved for demi-gods, which I am definitely not,* I thought. At this very moment, while I was trying to process a tornado inside of me, Paul opened his mouth and jokingly said, "We have quite some work to do, man."

Paul found this amusing, while my heart was being shattered. I laughed it off, not showing any emotion but ready to cry on the inside. It is difficult to describe the pain and distress I was feeling at that moment, about six months before my seventeenth birthday.

Right then, I realized that my aspirations and life purpose were simply vanishing. How the hell was I going to compete against these types of guys? I knew I couldn't.

I chose to ignore this realization and to keep living as if it never happened. Anyway, was there anything else than basketball all day, every day? No, there was not. Basketball, at the time, was the only thing on my mind and directing my whole life and my every move. Coming to terms with this realisation would have meant committing mental suicide. **I simply did not have the choice.**

Six Years Later

4:00 a.m., March 25, 2013
Fort Myers, Florida

Our team bus pulled up in front of Alico Arena, on our beautiful, palm tree-laden, tropical campus of Florida Gulf Coast University. Prior to boarding our chartered flight (courtesy of the NCAA), we had received pictures of what seemed like a giant party on campus. We could not wait to get back despite the late hour. We hoped our fellow students would stay up until we arrived. And staying up they did! A crowd of over 400 students and reporters had gathered in front of the gym, at 4:00 in the morning. Even for college students, this was too late to still be out chilling, and most definitely too early to wake up... Must have been a special occasion.

Indeed, it was.

They were all screaming, chanting, holding painted cardboards, and jumping on us as we descended from the team bus.

A few hours earlier, we upset Steve Fisher's San Diego State University in the round of 32 of the NCAA Tournament, the exact same stage of the tournament I had witnessed on TV almost six years earlier to the day, on March 19, 2007, in my hometown in Switzerland.

The fact that San Diego State's head coach was Steve Fisher, the legendary coach of Michigan's national championship team of 1989 and the Fab Five in 1991-92 only added more spice to the magic. (If you have not seen *The Fab Five*, the ESPN 30 for 30 documentary, get on it!)

NCAA Sweet 16, here we come! My stats: 11 points, 2 rebounds, 1 assist, 1 steal in 24 minutes of playing time, and a notable defensive performance on one of the fiercest competitors I had ever seen on the hardwood: Jamaal Franklin[2].

Don't believe the defensive part of it? Here is irrefutable proof!

Image 1:
Jamaal Franklin catches an alley-oop over me, 2013 NCAA Tournament, round of 32, Wells Fargo Center, Philadelphia.

---

[2] Jamaal Franklin was one of the top collegiate players of his generation. He was selected by the Memphis Grizzlies as the 41st pick of the 2013 NBA Draft, and has spent his career starring in China.

This game played out where my childhood hero, Allen Iverson, gave buckets and ankle-bullied so many, at the Wells Fargo Center, home of the Philadelphia 76ers. A few days earlier, we had made national news by upsetting Georgetown University (Iverson's alma mater) in the round of 64 of the tournament. That day, a crowd of over 20,000 fans was screaming and cheering for the underdog.

The comment of a reporter in a postgame interview:

"I have not seen this arena with as much energy since the 2001 NBA Finals..."

My magic moment:

Crossing the whole court, copying Allen Iverson's very own gesture—hand over the ear—in his own gym, to make our fans scream louder after San Diego State called a timeout to stop the flooding. What a moment.

That night was historic. On a personal level, I realized that my impossible dream ended up happening far beyond what I could ever have imagined. Most notably, we, the Florida Gulf Coast Eagles, became the lowest seed ever—15th seed—

Image 2:
Crossing the court and making the fans scream louder after San Diego State takes a timeout in the 2013 NCAA Tournament, round of 32, Wells Fargo Center, Philadelphia.

to reach the Round of 16 in the history of NCAA basketball. *(Equalled in 2021 by Oral Roberts University, and surpassed in 2022 by Saint Peter's University's magical Elite Eight run.)*

A Bit More About Myself

Before diving into the chapters of *The Basketball Path*, I would like to disclose a few more details about myself. I want to make sure you understand who I am and where I come from. Doing so will allow you to relate to my story as you go through this book and discover the principles that helped me turn my basketball journey from *impossible* to *I'm possible*.

In 2007, while watching the Kansas Jayhawks on TV, close to my 17th birthday, I stood at 6'1 ½" (186 cm) and weighed 145 pounds (65 kg). Do you expect me to say that by the time I got to college I added a few more inches?

Well, sorry to disappoint. My story is not the Paul George or Derrick White[3] fairy tale of an individual enjoying a four-inch late growth spurt. No. By the time I stepped off the bus at 4 a.m. on March 13, 2013, as a junior in college, I was still the same height and weighed 166 pounds (75.3 kg).

I am no exception. I am you. Mr. Regular with no physical advantage or secret talent. But through a great deal of dedication, some successes, and a lot of failures, I was able to make it further in basketball than most would even dream of.

---

[3] Paul George and Derrick White are both current NBA players. They both had a late growth spurt after 18 years old, which helped them elevate their game.

I did not reach all of my wildest basketball dreams, nor do I claim to have been a world class player. But I can confidently say that I lived an amazing basketball journey.

Representing my country both on the Juniors and Senior National team, earning a NCAA Division I full scholarship, being trusted to take the game winning shots and closing games at the free-throw line many times, being the sixth man in a team which reached the NCAA Sweet 16, scoring 42 points on national television against Baylor University, and enjoying calling basketball my job are just a few outcomes I was able to cherish as a player.

I promise you, none of it happened the easy way. I had to figure out unique ways to train and understand how to develop as a player to maximize my potential and have a chance to share the court with athletes much more gifted than me.

I have beat the odds big time in this basketball thing... and this book is here to help you take the same route. To get on this route, and understand precisely how this book can help you, there is one essential problematic to understand...

Players Are Let Down!

Overall, the youth basketball system is not built ideally for the long-term development of players. From very young, players play for wins, rankings, playoffs, and championships. This omnipresent competition affects both coaches and players.

On a first instance, coaches are "forced" to dedicate a lot of time working towards producing instant results, often failing to focus on long term development and educate players about the proper mindset to adopt for individual development.

On a second instance, this omnipresent competition affects the behavior of players who learn to worry about results very early in their playing days - *partly because of the education they receive from their coaches, and partly because it is simply human nature to do so* - instead of focusing on a long-term approach to training.

Even though many coaches hold the best intentions towards guiding players—offering good drills and advice as well as genuine interest in their future—by default, the main question on a coach's mind is: *How will I use my players with their current (or near future) skill set the best way possible to win games now, or within the next few months.?* This mindset creates a short-sight development approach, and the ones paying the price for it in the long term are the players.

I would like to make a side note to state that viewed from another angle, coaches who are focused on winning can actually benefit players even though they are looking for instant results. Winning is, to my knowledge, the most efficient and universal motivator there is. Winning at any age can really boost confidence, motivation, pleasure, and team chemistry, and as a result make players invest more effort into their game. Losing can quickly kill all of these, and lead to quitting. Focusing on winning games can therefore be beneficial when combined with a proper long-term development approach.

It is very important for players wishing for a basketball journey to understand this dynamic, and deduct one key thing from it: the responsibility to develop and harness one's full potential lies on themselves as players. This means helping their current and future teams be as competitive as possible, **developing more and better individual skills—tangible and intangible—in line with their own profile, for their coaches to use now and in the future.**

And here is exactly where the problematic lies: expecting players to take on this responsibility without receiving proper education, guidance and knowledge about talent development, game understanding and all the other things that help form a great player is simply setting them up for failure. Sensible personal development is too complex of a task to handle without a proper support system.

Here is the real gap, the reason why most players waste so much potential, only to realize later how much they could have ... if they would have [...fill in the blank].

Millions of dollars are spent each season by high budget teams and high salary players to hire sport's psychologists, athlete's counselors, special player's development coaches and the likes.

The Basketball Path was written to make top-notch guidance accessible to all, helping players take responsibility for their development, as well as providing parents and coaches the knowledge and tools to guide their players toward lasting success.

Bridge the Gap – What this Book will Give You

What I propose in this book is two-folds. In first instance, I will share with you the different mindsets and concepts players need to learn and adopt to develop in line with their own profile, for best long-term results.

It is easy to preach, and tell others what to do. After all, each of us has a 20/20 hindsight... This is why I wanted to go further than simply giving retrospect advice to the next generation.

In second instance, I will propose a way to wrap all the teaching of the book in an easy to use system that I call the MyStride Approach. Using this system will help you harness the tremendous power of deliberately choosing your actions moment after moment.

This book is designed to help players from the outside-in, providing a path to follow in line with their profile, while helping them understand the team's sphere and coaches' expectations to perform in the present, all while developing for best long-term results.

By applying this book's teachings and the MyStride Approach, you can expect to gain an invaluable mental edge; become more accountable for yourselves, gain **structure in your practices *and in life*, increase your efficiency and consistency, and elevate your self-consciousness in practices and games.**

To help you get the most out of this book and take actions in your life, we have created a *Basketball Path* workbook. You can easily find it for download at *www.strideyourpassion.com/services*.

Note:
throughout the book, the explanations and the implementation of the MyStride Approach will be specifically targeted for basketball training. However, its key principles are transferable and adaptable to any activity, from sport to music to everyday life. From football to violin to schoolwork. Feel free to adapt!

How this Book Came to Life and What's to Come

At the age of 14, I started to dedicate most of my time and energy to the game of basketball, sacrificing anything that stood in the way. Twelve years later, at 26 years old, basketball got taken away from me.... After years of chronic pain on my knees, my body would not take the toll anymore. (*I would have to undergo four surgeries and four years of recurrent pain before feeling good enough to play sports again!*)

Coming back to the game was not an option anymore. I did not know what to do. I was lost...

On a personal level, I needed a change... The problem was, I did not know *how* to change or *what* to change. Just when I needed it the most, I met Stefan (*they say that when the student is ready, the teacher appears),* a life adventurer who had defied the odds in his own field. He mentored me for over a year in applying some of the concepts and tricks he had learned while studying productivity and personal development for many years, reading through countless books and experimenting with a long process of trial and error. His teachings changed my life.

I quickly recognized how much the concepts and methods Stefan shared with me would have benefitted me in my basketball and life journey. I went to work, adapting what I learned, mixing it with my personal knowledge and basketball experience to create something that would help players develop their game.

The MyStride Approach was born. In 2019, I started working with my first client, and then another one. After a few months and the amazing results obtained with the half dozen players I was working with, I decided to put it all into pages.

I thought a few months was all I needed to finish this book project... months turned to years and this "book project" turned in to the (second) most profound, humbling, challenging, frustrating and rewarding journey of my life.

I promise you that I poured everything I had in this book and wrote it with full sincerity and honesty.

I hope my work will give you something positive to implement – or something negative to take away – In the way you approach the game *and life.* (Oh, yeah.. the biggest project of my life? My basketball journey. Nothing will ever surpass the work and emotional investment I put into basketball.)

Just like a basketball game, this book is divided into four quarters. You just went through the warmup and are now in the pregame huddle.

During the First Quarter, we will get into rhythm by exploring seven principles that are essential to understand, integrate, and apply to become a good player.

In the Second Quarter, we will focus on understanding the three pillars the MyStride Approach is built upon.

Engaging on this basketball journey does not come without its hurdles. In the Third Quarter, we will talk about the dangers and pitfalls anyone dreaming of basketball will inevitably go through and how to overcome them.

In the Fourth Quarter, with all the prerequisite background knowledge in mind, we will look into the practical step-by-step implementation of the MyStride Approach. This part, if correctly implemented with the knowledge gained throughout the book, can and will change your life.

The last part of the book will be the Overtime section. In it, I will disclose the real journeys of basketball players and their path to a professional career. As you will see, many have faced and overcame adversity to reach their dreams. I will also share insightful and inspirational quotes I have gathered throughout my own journey. When in need of a boost, you will always be able to return to that section and renew your strength and motivation to get back at it.

I am beyond delighted to begin this journey with you. Let's go.

FIND RHYTHM

"A principle is a principle and in no case can it be watered down because of our incapacity to live it in practice.
We have to strive to achieve it, and the striving should be conscious, deliberate, and hard."

—MAHATMA GANDHI

As discussed in the Warm-Up, **the responsibility to actualize your potential lies on yourself and no one else.** Throughout the book, I will always be talking about actualizing your given potential, and will never talk about actual level of playing. As we will see, we are not all created equal in terms of talent, natural abilities, or specific pre-dispositions. Some people are born with phenomenal gifts for basketball and will reach higher levels than others while putting in similar or even less effort. For the vast majority of us, there is no choice but to tap into our maximum potential to have a fighting chance at reaching the heights we wish for ourselves. And I believe it is just right.

Reaching the maximum of one's potential in a sport or any other activity one loves is probably the greatest feeling of accomplishment anyone can experience. Think about it: are you more grateful for and proud of the things you attained through hard work, sweat and tears, or the things that were given to you freely? (I thought so too.)

What is beautiful and rewarding is the long journey of pursuing a passion, what one learns about himself and about the world along the way, and the internal knowledge that the maximum effort was given to truly pursue and live this passion. As my college teammate and dear friend Charlie "Buckets" Little[4] would say back in the day, "The journey is the reward."

To excel at any activity you will need time and effort—and much more.... I believe there are seven utmost important mindsets, or principles, to understand and apply to get the most out of practice time and progress faster. Throughout this whole First Quarter, I will go into depth with each of them. Understanding and integrating these principles is an essential place to start in order to fully grasp and implement the MyStride Approach. Think of these mindsets as pieces of software to download and run in the back of your mind at all times.

---

[4] If you like sneakers, follow my former teammate and YouTube star Charlie "Buckets" and his brother on the best sneaker channel there is on YouTube and Instagram: @mrfoamersimpson

Principle 1: Think Systems

"I think it's very important to have a feedback loop, where you're constantly thinking about what you've done and how you could be doing it better. I think that's the single best piece of advice: constantly think about how you could be doing things better and questioning yourself."

—ELON MUSK

Throughout the years, I have seen countless players who had talent, high-level ambitions, and strong intentions to reach their hoop dreams. They weren't lazy. They worked hard, they invested a lot...and they never became good enough to reach their goals. How come? Having goals and working hard at it is the key to success, right?

Wrong. This is a myth.

Imagine yourself having a bow and arrow, and trying to hit a target while being blindfolded, while not knowing where the target is. Blindfolded, one can know what he is shooting for and have all the best intentions in the world, but he will have no idea if he is aiming and shooting in the right direction, nor will he receive feedback to adjust his aim for the next try... This, with slight exaggeration, is how most of us are taught to go after our aspirations. It is also exactly how most young players advance when dreaming to play basketball at the next level.

Unfortunately, our schools and parents don't properly teach us about goals and dreams and how to make them real when we grow up. They focus on making us believe we can become whatever we wish to become, but they fail to teach us the right methodology to achieve a desired outcome. They fail either on purpose because they don't want us to truly follow our dreams (preferring we take a more traditional and safe route), or by accident because they actually lack knowledge about how to attain objectives.

Players know what they want. They want outcomes and results—to become a starter, get more playing time, play professionally, play in college, etc... These are outcome goals. They sound great and offer energy and motivation, but are not helping players advance in a specific direction day after day.

To reach a destination or achieve a goal, simply wanting it is not enough. Knowing how to get to it and applying and fine-tuning this knowledge are the real tasks at hand. A destination can only be reached one step at a time. The attention must therefore shift away from the outcome and be refocused towards defining and applying the processes that lead to it over time—the very definition of systems.

The driver and GPS analogy further illustrates this concept: when driving to a new destination, turning on the navigation system is a wise thing to do. The software will calculate the different road options in the backend, and propose a route. Following and applying the directions allows you to focus solely on the task at hand (turning left, making a U-turn, taking the next exit), while knowing that each of these small actions are taking you a step closer to the desired destination.

You may have noticed that in this analogy, a destination is required for the GPS to propose a route. Similarly, designing and applying a sensible basketball system requires a destination to be defined. Outcome goals, as we already discussed, are not good destinations to aim for: they are brief, not fully controllable, and often change over time. They should therefore never be mistaken to be end destinations. So, where should players with ambitions set their destination to?

Although outcome goals may differ from player to player, the true destination any motivated player is after is very similar. The thread to follow and be guided by is the **fulfillment and maximization of the individual potential**.

By shifting from a vague desired outcome far off in the future, *such as playing professionally*, to understanding that the end destination and the highest point someone can reach is the maximization of his or her given potential—*which in turn will increase the chances to reach any outcome, oftentimes exceeding one's wildest expectations*—players can design and build **individualized** "navigation" systems that will help focus on the processes, and offer constant feedback, much like a GPS does.

Goals are not all bad. Formulated the proper way, and within systems, they can be really helpful. We will see exactly how in the fourth quarter's step by step implementation of the MyStride Approach. For now, focus on understanding the main message of this first principle: **systems help you focus on the moment-to-moment processes, and provide you with constant feedback on whether you are getting closer to your target or farther away from it.**

Designing and following a thoughtful system, or as Elon Musk says "a feedback loop," is the best way to get the most out of the cards you were dealt and achieving special outcomes.

Principle 2: Understand Your Profile

"Now is no time to think of what you do not have. Think of what you can do with that there is."

—Ernest Hemmingway

Dictionary definition of "potential": *The latent qualities or abilities that may be developed and lead to future success or usefulness.*

The individual potential of a participant in any activity, whether it is basketball, music, math, or anything else, stems from the combination of multiple factors.

Leaving socio-economic, cultural, or geographical factors out of the picture, I believe there are three main factors to consider when determining someone's potential in a particular field:

- Talent
- Physical predispositions
- Work ethic/effort

I will not elaborate deeply on this subject as it is not the purpose of this book, but it is a concept very important to understand for later purposes. Let's quickly define each of these three factors:

- **TALENT** is how easily one can learn and assimilate a particular activity or subject. It's how naturally the activity comes to the person. As Angela Duckworth clearly puts it in her book *Grit*[5], talent is how quickly skills improve when one invests effort. Applied to basketball, it means

---

[5] Angela Duckworth, *Grit: The Power of Passion and Perseverance* (New York: Scribner, 2016).

how fast someone can assimilate movements, understand concepts, improve coordination, and get an overall feel for the ball and the game; how naturally the game comes to the player. Digging further into the concept, talent can be divided into subcategories: tangibles (ball handling, shooting, overall technique) and intangibles (placements, game IQ, leadership, etc...). For the purpose of an easy explanation, we will only talk about talent without referring to any specific subcategory.

- **PHYSICAL PREDISPOSITION** is how well-adapted the person's phenotype and physical attributes are to the specific activity. A swimmer's perfect body is different from a basketball player's perfect body and is different from a jockey's perfect body. **Physical predisposition has a lot to do with genetics and is often mistakenly believed to be the sole indicator of how much potential one has.** In the case of basketball, a great physical pre-dispositioned player would be around 6'6" (198 cm) or more, blessed with great motor control and good explosiveness. A low physical predisposition player would be one who is un-explosive and of small size. *Everything else being equal,* the player with better physical predisposition for a given activity will outperform the other one.

Note: For mental activities like writing, math, and chess, the line between talent and physical predisposition is blurry. One could argue that they interlink. Everyone has a different brain structure, and looking into it closely would certainly reveal natural neuronal pathways that predispose for certain types of activities.

From birth, a gifted mathematician's brain will be structurally different from a gifted lyricist's brain, which predisposes them into excelling in a certain field.

Is specific brain structure responsible for creating talent in physical activities too? Is talent simply a specific arrangement of brain synapses and nerve connections, being in fact an integral part of predisposition? I don't know. It may be, as our movements, perceptions, and interaction with the world are directed mostly from the brain and its nervous system.

In this book, we are talking and focusing on a physical sport, so let's keep talent and predisposition separated.

- **WORK ETHIC/EFFORT.** I use the term *work ethic* in a broad sense, in which passion and love are included. Essentially, how much is a player going to give to his activity on a day-to-day basis? How much effort is put into the vocation he chooses? Not only the effort given at practice, but also the emotional investment into the sport or activity.

To paraphrase Angela Duckworth again: When talent mixes with effort, the results are skills. When those acquired skills are combined with effort, achievement results.

These two sentences can be turned into a simple equation:

Talent × Effort = Skill

Skill × Effort = Achievement[6]

---

[6] Duckworth, Angela. 2016. *Grit: The Power of Passion and Perseverance.* New York, NY: Scribner.

I will let you reflect on this equation before coming back to it in the conclusion of this principle.

The three components we just talked about—talent, predisposition, and work ethic—can be illustrated by the following graphic:

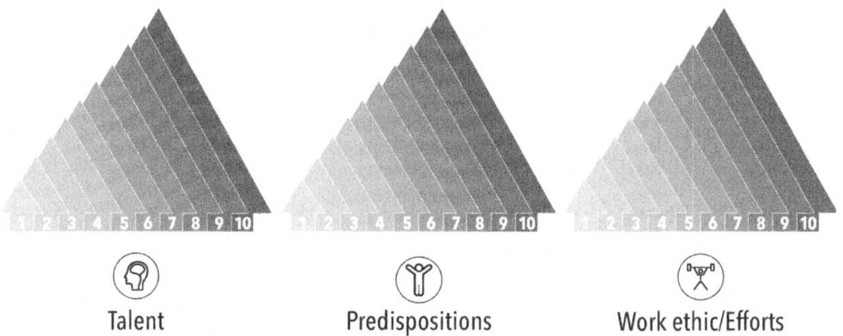

Image 3: Profile scale.

Any basketball player will fall somewhere on each of these scales. Knowing where you stand is a great start. As we will see at the beginning of the Second Quarter, self-knowledge and awareness are very important on the journey towards improvement.

For now, let's explore this concept by looking at a few different combinations of these three characteristics in players we all know. Please keep in mind that the scale I use for the following players is very harsh. It is against fellow NBA players. Rating physical predispositions next to Giannis Antetokounmpo[7] will make even some professional players rate below a 2 out of 10. When doing this exercise, it is important to judge yourself on an appropriate scale.

---

[7] Giannis Antetokounmpo, "The Greek Freak," is a two-time NBA MVP who led the Milwaukee Bucks to the 2021 NBA championship.

Kevin Durant (KD)[8]:

Talent: 9.5. Sky-high talent, KD has an amazing natural touch, understanding of the game, scoring instinct, and great timing.

Physical predisposition: 9.5. Long frame, great motor skills (very mobile and agile with his body), off-the-charts wingspan. The reason why I am not giving him a 10 is for his lack of physical strength. However, this small subtraction does not hurt him much because his physique actually compliments his style of play (and vice versa). *(Side note: Give KD a 6'2" (188 cm) frame, keeping all else equal, and I am ready to bet that he would not be playing in the NBA).*

Work ethic: 9. We have all heard stories of KD staying late at night in the gym; we have seen him working with special coaches, perfecting moves in the offseason. KD loves the game, enjoys spending time in the gym, and uses each day to perfect his already above-level skills. Because we all know Kobe (RIP and thank you, Kobe), KD cannot receive a 10 in this category.

Scoring high in all three categories in your field of interest, as KD does, is like winning the lottery. It is a gift from nature. This is why there are so few incredible superstars—perfect prototypes to play this game. When scoring this high across the board, only injuries, prison, drugs and alcohol, or being a complete a**hole can keep you away from a promising future. (More high potential players than you think fall into one or more of these tragic dead ends).

---

[8] Kevin Durant is a former NBA MVP, a two-time NBA champion, and a four-time NBA scoring champion.

Let's look at another player. A player who was, and in my opinion not legitimately, criticized in the past. He nonetheless enjoyed a 9-year NBA career during which he won a title, and represented his country in 3 Olympic games.

Matthew "Delly" Dellavedova[9]:

Talent: 7. Yes, 7! He may not be flashy like Kyrie Irving, but Dellavadova has an incredible feel for the game, has great vision, and knows how and what to do on the floor to be effective. He scores way above average in game IQ and can see things on the floor that many cannot.

Physical predispositions: 3. Compared to the likes of LeBron, Anthony Davis, and Zion Williamson, I give the Aussie a very small 3 out of 10. In the NBA, a league where most players are some of the greatest athletes in the world, he stands way below the vast majority of them. (Keep in mind, Dellavadova scores a 3 against the top basketball athletes in the world, but compare him to the general population and the scale would be different).

Work ethic: 9. Extreme. Simply, the efforts it takes to compete day in and day out against guys who are stronger and faster means he can never take a break on the floor and always has to work and play at 200% intensity to have a fighting chance. This is also why he suffered many injuries in the past few years.

A close friend of mine from Australia attended the AIS (Australian Institute of Sport), a place where the top

---

[9] Matthew "Delly" Dellavedova was undrafted. He played in the NBA from 2013 to 2020. He now represents Melbourne United in the NBL.

Aussie athletes of each sport train. He told me that one Saturday there was a celebration night when the whole basketball team got dressed, ready to go out, but they could not find Delly. After looking through the dorms and calling his cell phone without success, they headed to the courts. They found him shooting free throws alone and running sprints after each miss…at 11:00 p.m.

This player profile analysis is very simplified. In the Fourth Quarter, we will use a far more comprehensive tool to analyse yourself as a player. The aim now is firstly to understand that knowing your profile will allow you to work on your game accordingly, and secondly, to become aware of the following two points:

- **Effort is the key to any achievement.** An easy conclusion can be made from Angela Duckworth's equations; someone with less talent might take longer or require more effort to acquire skills and yet again more time and effort to turn these skills into achievement. But low-effort input, even with high talent, will stand no chance of reaching anything significant. Many had the same talent and same predispositions as your favorite NBA or Euro League players, but neither you nor I have ever heard of them.
- **Effort is the only parameter a player has full control over.** Talent and predisposition, are determined by your genetic background, prenatal environment, early education, and a bunch of other factors you had and currently have no control over. Effort is a choice, a commitment anyone can deliberately make.

Everyone has a ceiling, but if the proper ladder is used to reach it, most will find that it is much higher than they thought. Effort and work ethic, **applied the right way**, is the key to reaching your full potential based on the cards you have been dealt.

It is now time to look into yourself: the regular, or not so regular, guy or girl, impassioned by the game. Where do you stand in the three metrics we just talked about?

WORKBOOK EXERCISE I – 3 METRICS

(find the *Basketball Path* workbook to download for free at www.strideyourpassion.com/services)

My advice: Be careful with the scale you use. Compare yourself to players in your league. If you are a club player, look where you stand compared to other club-level players. If you are in regional teams, or area rankings, look at the guys at this level. If you are at the national team level, compare yourself to the other guys on the national team. The goal is not to compare yourself to unrealistic objectives like Vince Carter or Kyrie Irving, which would make most of us score very low, nor to compare yourself with players way below your level in order to look like an all-star.

My Talent

Grade: ..../10

How naturally does the game come to you (tangible & intangible)?

....

....

....

My Predispositions

Grade: ....../10

How well do your physical attributes fit the sport of basketball?

....

....

....

My Work Ethic

Grade: ....../10

How much are you giving to the game? What is the craziest thing you have done for basketball?

....

....

....

Principle 3: Give Love and Passion

"The most powerful weapon on earth is the human soul on fire."

—Ferdinand Foch

The third metric of Principle 2, *work ethic and effort*, is of such importance that I decided to make it a principle in itself. Because in reality, it is about much more than work ethic and effort.

We have all been fascinated by jaw-dropping performances of past and current superstars. We have all sat in front of a computer screen on YouTube after typing "Pistol Pete" Maravich, Jason Williams, Jamal Crawford, Kobe Bryant, Kyrie Irving, or Trae Young highlights and watched in disbelief some of the moves executed.

All these mind-blowing moves, the feel and the instinct for the game those players showcase is not just the result of hard work and effort... It is the result of much more than that. A deep obsessional love for the game and for the ball. Hard and smart work is good; it gets results. But pure passion, pure love makes one go beyond the notion of hard work.

A player who dearly loves and has passion for the art of basketball will think about his movements all day, and will even practice in his sleep. It will be all he thinks about, for most of the day and night. When true passion is alive, training never stops and the compounding results can be astonishing over time.

I call it love. You can call it obsession, passion, or any other name.... No matter who you are, and no matter where you are from, this is the type of relationship with the game of basketball you must have if you wish to reach your full potential as a player.

Passion and love are what will make one give the necessary effort, sustain the heartbreaking failures, stay motivated through gruesome and painful injuries, work harder when getting benched, and keep the hope alive when nothing goes the right way. It is the driving force behind any player relentlessly pushing towards their basketball dream and beyond their limits.

Don't get me wrong: Someone can become a good basketball player or even a professional player, even in some cases an NBA player, while not being deeply in love with the game. There are many who made careers simply because they were very athletic, because they were extremely talented, or were a combination of both. But no one can and no one will ever reach their full basketball potential if they are not in love with the game.

Hasheem Thabeet was the No. 2 overall pick in the 2009 NBA Draft. He was drafted at 21 years old, only six years after having started playing basketball. He was 7'3" (221 cm) and could run like a gazelle and block shots. He had an incredibly high potential ceiling. One thing was sure, he was the next big thing. Or was he? Hasheem never came close to reaching his promised potential. Many reports and articles online describe Hasheem's lack of dedication towards basketball excellence.

Looking back at the player I was that very night of 2007, watching my first NCAA March Madness game at 16 years old,

I would not have bet a dime on myself that one day I would get paid to play basketball. But love for the game I had.

I started playing close to my eighth birthday. I really liked it. But it was around 14 years old that the virus hit me. Around that time, I declined taking part in all my previous activities—tennis, ski weekends, any school trip that would make me miss a practice, and even family vacations that did not have a basketball court option included. No court? Not going. None of those would help me get to where I aimed to go. Basketball was the subject of quite a few heated family conversations, but I always fought for my love, never relenting a single inch for it.

Each passing year, my love and passion for the game would grow stronger and I would do bolder things to spend more time playing basketball and perfecting my movements.

At 14, I went to the janitor of a local basketball gym in my town to try to get the keys. I had my mom and a coach backing me up for credibility, and I offered to clean the gym whenever needed in exchange for that key. Luckily, he finally gave me the key without the cleaning included in the deal.

I spent so much time in there, training alone or with a friend on Saturdays and Sundays, from 14 years old until I left for the US at 18, that anytime a rubber-like smell hits my nostrils, my mind is directly transported to the joy and the cries of the grind, alone in my green-rubber-floor gym.

At Worcester Academy, my first year in the US, the gyms were closed after 7 p.m. on the weekends. I would make sure to go in right before the automatic locking of the doors, and tie a tie (yes, a tie because it was the closest thing I had to a rope) around the doorknob system to ensure that the door could not lock. I would then go train alone until school curfew at midnight.

Since there were windows, I would keep the lights off and play in the dark so the security guards or school faculty wouldn't catch me. The only light in the gym was the red emergency EXIT sign, and sometimes a bit of moonlight. Once the eyes got used to it, the rim was just perceivable enough for me to guess where it was. The dangerous part was to let the ball stop bouncing after a miss. It gets scary searching for a ball in a quiet pitch-dark corner.

One day, someone removed the tie from the door and I found myself locked out and unable to train. I went back to the dorms and started to practice ball handling in the kitchen on the ground floor, at 10 p.m. I remember the faculty on duty that night appearing through the door and looking at me, shirt off and sweating as I bounced the ball through my drills, in complete disbelief. He did not know if he should punish me or not. He finally left, saying that I was completely out of my mind. It came from the bottom of his heart.

I did those things because there was no other place I'd rather be. It was fueled by love. And this is the reason why I ended up having a fighting chance competing throughout my basketball journey.

Any of the players you see excelling on the floor have been through countless unseen hours working on their craft, sometimes in unorthodox and unconventional manners that can only come from love and passion.

Jimmer Fredette, the sensational Brigham Young University star who later played in the NBA, China and Europe, used to dribble outside on an uneven concrete ground with construction gloves on his hands as a teenager. He and his family also organized basketball games in the local penitentiary to get him used to a more physical style of basketball.

Kobe Bryant would work out at 5 a.m. when he was in high school. He kept going with the same mentality even after being an all-star. Multiple accounts describe him working on his game with the left hand only when his right hand was injured, being found in full sweat in the gym at 4:30 in the morning by staff members, watching film at halftime of games, and many more other things that most people would call crazy.

Legendary skater Tony Hawk recounts that his dad would have to physically get him out of the skating bowl to go home as he simply would not leave until certain tricks would be mastered.

When he was a child, Wayne Gretzky would watch NHL games with a piece of blank paper and a pen, and without taking his eyes off the screen, he would draw the path of the puck on his paper. When the game would finish, the paper would show darker areas where the puck would most often be. Wayne would go on to ultra-dominate the hockey scene and display puck control and anticipation like the world has never seen. He is to this day considered the greatest hockey player of all time.

Growing up in the 60's, Seve Ballesteros owned only one golf club. An old 3 iron his brother had gifted him. Being from a modest family, he wasn't able to play on the local Pedreña Golf Club. He would spend entire days (sometimes missing school) on the sand of the vast Atlantic beaches of Pedreña, Spain, with his 3 iron club and a few balls, practicing shots and making up his own holes. The only time he could enter the golf club to practice was at night—in fraud—by jumping over the fences and playing under the moonlight. Seve grew to become one of the most influential golfers of his era, ranked as the world's #1 golfer multiple times, and was admired for his unmatched creativity with a golf club in his hands.

I could find hundreds of similar stories, from sports to art to business, of people who seem to play in a league above everyone else. But when digging slightly deeper, the secret gets spilled. It is the unmatched love and passion of these individuals that allowed them to push themselves and reach levels of mastery that seemed unreachable.

A deep, uncontrollable love and passion for the game is necessary to tap into your basketball potential and become the player you can become, given the cards you were dealt. It is what will make you invest the necessary time and energy to master your craft and push through the obstacles that will inevitably arise on your path.

How much do you love the game? What is the craziest thing you have done for the game? I would love to hear your crazy stories. Share them with me at **basketballpath@gmail.com**

Principle 4: Make'em Count

"The will to win is important, but the will to prepare is vital."

—JOE PATERNO

Passion and love for a basketball player is just like fuel to a plane. It provides energy. Fuel feeds the engines to make the plane go as fast as possible and get off the ground. However, it does not direct it. For a plane to take off, and arrive at a destination, it needs a knowledgeable pilot. Unless a player learns how to direct and fly the plane, he will never reach his desired destination, no matter how full his tanks or how powerful his engines are.

All training should be a preparation to comfortably perform in a game. It is therefore wisest to extend the range of comfort by risking and experiencing failure in practice, to then benefit from a wider range of comfort when competition time comes. The players who understand this possess an incredible advantage over the others. They understand exactly the reason why things are done a certain way instead of simply going through the motions. As a result, practice time is invested, not spent.

If your skills were delimited by a boundary, you must spend as much practice time as possible with one foot in-bounds and one foot out-of-bounds, juggling between the two. Slowly, the comfort zone will expand and you will continuously overcome what was previously challenging, as illustrated in image 4 below.

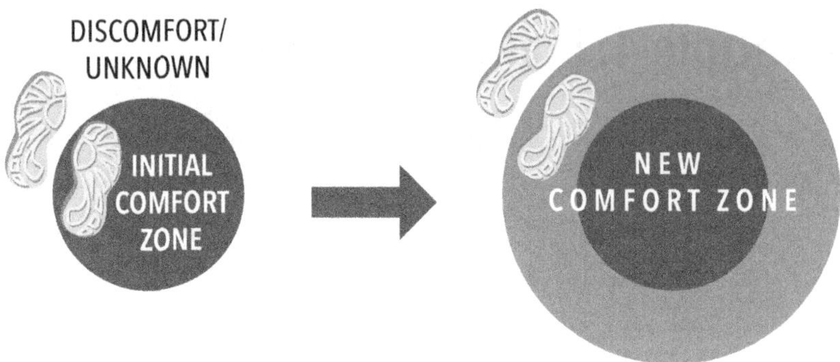

Image 4: Growing the comfort zone

Knowing how to work this way is a skill set. And the good news is, like any other skill, it can be learned. Find below a list of personal responsibilities concerning different aspects of the game that players can and should adhere to at practice to take advantage of each moment and grow their comfort zone.

SHOOTING: Perfecting your shot in ways that will maximize your in-game shooting percentage. Here are a few ways to achieve this, whether by yourself or within the team sphere.

- Perfecting the form instead of worrying about making baskets.
- Working on a faster, higher and more efficient release instead of staying comfortable with a lower and slower release.
- Working consciously on different footwork and situations on the catch.
- Imagining a defender closing out.

Most players worry about making the most shots possible during practice, which as a result keeps them within their shooting comfort zone. With this mindset, improvement and performance are plateaued and game performance suffers over the long term.

I have come across countless players who were able to shoot the ball unbelievably well during practice but were unable to make a bucket in games because the shots they'd take in games had to be much faster and with more intensity than the shots they would take while practicing. The result was a lack of confidence and frequently missed shots or, even worse, passed-up shooting opportunities.

If your game shots feel different than your practice shots, it means you are not practicing the right way.

BALL HANDLING AND PASSING: Always imagine a mighty defender standing in front of you. Players often go through the motions and believe that they will be ready once live play starts. Just like shooting, if the right habits are not perfected during practice, failure is likely to happen.

UNDERSTANDING THE VALUE OF TIME: Time is limited. As a basketball player, you do not have 40 years' time to develop like it is the case in other careers. You therefore must understand time's precious value.

Ten minutes before practice, fifteen minutes after practice, or even five minutes during the water break will add up over time. If you are a normal person with responsibilities on the side such as school, homework, a side job, friends, family duties, and other hobbies, these precious minutes count. Ten minutes per day, six times per week, adds up to fifty-two hours in a year.

How many floaters (or any other movement) can you do in fifty-two hours? I estimate I can get between 10 and 15 floaters up per minute, depending on how I do it. By going slow, at the rate of 10 per minute, this adds up to 31,200 repetitions in a year.

Do you think your muscle memory, floaters accuracy, and technique will improve after taking over thirty thousand reps?

On the flip side, if you spend on average one hour per day (and most spend more than that) either scrolling through social media, or playing video games, this one hour which seems like nothing will add up to a total of 365 hours over a year. This is equivalent to spending a full month of 30 days, eyes glued on the screen 12 hours per day. I will let you calculate the opportunity cost...

Hebb's Law

In neuroscience, Hebb's Law is a theory stating that when neurons repeatedly fire together, their synaptic connections strengthen.

To understand Hebb's Law is key in the apprenticeship of any sport, movement or activity. Our brain is an incredible machine of adaptation. It is literally made to adapt to the environment and activities presented to it. Initially, acquiring a skill requires undivided focus and attention. If repeated and experienced enough times, the brain will create neural-connections and pathways providing the person with the ability to perform it better and faster while consuming less resources over time.

Hebb's law is at work at all times, and can both reinforce good or bad movements and reflexes. This is why it is so important to consciously perform the proper fundamentals from the start. Once a movement is repeated many times, the neural-pathways become strong and hard to break. We often see amateur practitioners who picked up a sport for fun, without proper focus put on fundamentals, playing or competing with awful mechanics and being unable to change them. After so many repetitions executed the wrong way, fixing them would first require unlearning, a task far more difficult than learning properly from the start.

The key in learning any movement or skill is to try to bring it from conscious to unconscious, from making many mistakes to flowing effortlessly, from high awareness of the movement to an automatic reflex by **repeating it enough times the proper way** for the brain to create the right and useful connections. To picture how powerful this is, and how much can be achieved through this concept, think about walking. Today, you most likely walk without thinking twice about it. As a matter of fact, walking is probably so easy to you that you can perform very advanced tasks in parallel (like dribbling a basketball between the legs, being aware of the defense, and thinking about the next play).

But walking on two feet is a very complex task. Our brain has to take care of so many things, from space awareness to balance to activating the right muscles. Think about how much time and practice it took you to learn how to walk effortlessly. If you are a normal human, it took you between 10 and 14 months just to be able to take your first few steps, and another year or more to feel confident about walking. Each time you tried, your brain recorded the information and built stronger and stronger neural pathways and muscle memory.

Luckily for us, very few skills are as hard to perform and as complex as walking. However, the process of learning a skill stays the same. To become elite at something, we have to start by doing it consciously and repeat it enough times for our amazing brain to create the necessary connections to make it natural and effortless.

When I was playing, my specialty was that I could shoot with a very fast trigger and with high accuracy. People around me always talked about the natural gift I had to shoot the ball. But what they did not understand is that each shot (pre-practice, in practice, and post-practice) was shot with the clear intention to have the fastest trigger possible, or to broaden my footwork.

While others (not many) took as many reps as I did, their focus was often to make the basket instead of developing specific ways to create a more effective shot. Over time, Hebb's Law took care of things and put me in a category apart in terms of shooting the basketball.

GOAT Stephen Curry took it to another level. His shooting became so natural that it seems like the ball is an extension of his body. Trust me, this did not happen overnight, nor did it happen by chance...

Smart players understand the value of each repetition. Know how to use each moment to your advantage and understand the value of each shot, each dribble, each offensive and defensive possession, each minute on the court, from the layup lines to the 5-on-5s. Make'em count.

Principle 5: Visualize

"Mental rehearsal is just as important as physical rehearsal."
—Phil Mickelson

He can smell the atmosphere in the gym. He carries himself with assurance and confidence. His body is in full awareness mode, and he can feel all of his muscles working in concert as they contract and relax to move efficiently and effortlessly. The ball is in his hands and he can see the game in slow motion, using and creating the spaces needed to perfection. He squares off the defender and attacks the basket going to the right; plants his left foot to stop on a dime, and raises graciously into the air for a pull-up as the defender tries in vain to contest the shot. He feels his body twisting and his right leg extending in front, slightly to the left as his body unfolds to square off his shoulders. His wrist releases the ball over the defense. *Squouwshhh.* Thank you, Kobe, for showing the way.

It is 2:30 a.m., and he has been playing basketball nonstop for about five hours. He is going against his opponents full sway, but does not feel any physical fatigue. He is still as lucid as ever, making play after play as both team's supporters watch the show in awe. The only drawback is that his alarm will ring in about four hours for school and he is still wide awake.

You guessed it. He is still playing the game way into the late hours of the night, tucked in his bed. While most are asleep, his mind is still on the court, and his body can feel all the sensations. He is going through every good play he can remember from the earlier game, and replaying bad plays hundreds of times over, exploring all the choices and scenarios that could have played out differently...and in the process he gains experience, skills, and more...

It is scientifically proven that the same neural pathways activate when we *think* about performing a movement as when actually performing it. Thinking about movements, visualizing them, feeling them through our whole being is almost as powerful as actually physically doing them. Using this knowledge and understanding that progress does not happen only on the floor is essential.

Most believe that practice starts when they lace their shoes, and ends when they take them off... that access to gyms and personal coaches is key to accumulating moves and techniques. The truth is, a big portion of the work can and must be done mentally.

All basketball movements are sourced from your brain. It sends commands to and through your nervous system for your body to execute them. Activating, strengthening and creating these pathways is what is at work when rehearsing mentally.

The potential impact of mental imagery is huge. Here are a few other proven benefits that derive from it:

- Muscle mass can be sustained on an immobilized injured body part by merely imagining doing exercises.
- A whole array of cognitive processes; motor control, attention, perception, and memory to name a few, are all positively impacted by mental imagery.

If mere imagination can create those types of changes in muscle building or cognitive abilities, just think about how powerful and how much effect a well-run and adequate visualization and mental practice can have on your overall game: on your shooting, ball-handling, finishes around the basket, and even on your decision making or your confidence on the floor.

Visualization can and will help you exploit your full potential. However, it is important to do it well to reap the benefits of it.

We have worked with professional meditation teachers to create a set of guided visualizations and meditations to help players develop their games through proper mental work. The meditations are focused on different subjects, such as shooting, game confidence, pre-game mental preparation and more... You can access them directly on **www.strideyourpassion.com/services**, and start your journey in mental work and mindfulness.

For those wishing to do it alone, here is a quick step-by step to help you structure your visualization work:

- Get to a comfortable, quiet place and relax (sitting or lying down).
- Close your eyes and take a few deep breaths to help your body get to a state of meditation. (*You access a meditative state when your brain emits Alpha waves... this is why it is always better to be guided through it when you start.*)
- Start to feel the environment around you. Are you at practice or in competition? Home or away? How does the gym look?
- See and feel yourself performing and acting the way you want to. See the images of yourself both through your own eyes and through an external camera.

- Engage as many senses as possible. What are you wearing? What do you see around you? Is there a specific smell you can recall? What do you hear? How does your body feel?
- Rehearse specific situations on the court.
- Immerse yourself in the positive emotions you get from playing or training well.

Visualization is something you can easily take responsibility for, given that you can do it almost anywhere at any time. Integrate it as part of your practice time, and work on it as you would with any other basketball skill. With practice, you will get better at it. Done the right way, it will allow you to create and consolidate your neural pathways and help your movements and perception of the game become faster, more automatic, and more accurate.

Principle 6: Recognize the OGs

*"I can lead the horse to water, but I cannot make him drink. It's just a b**** when the dehydrated horse tells you later he should have had a drink."*

—Unknown

Those who did it all alone, you have never heard of. They have never made it.

All top athletes have had key people on their side offering inspiration, guidance, mentorship, and much more along the way.

Humans have a unique capacity to share and pass down knowledge. Each generation benefits from the previous one's experience and teachings to reach new heights. It took Thomas Edison[10], one of the great scientific minds of modern history, years of work and thousands of tries not to invent the light bulb, but to improve on the versions of his predecessors. Even one of the greatest inventors to ever live relied on prior knowledge as well as constant collaboration of his peers.

Likewise, through sharing, basketball evolved a great deal. Today, some high school players are more skilled than superstars were back in the day. This is only possible thanks to all the work done and all the knowledge that has been passed down from previous generations.

In urban slang, OGs are people who helped pave the way and lead and inspire either a few individuals or entire generations. The term stands for "Original Gangster". Ancient

---

[10] Thomas Edison was a prolific inventor and the founder of General Electric. He is often credited for inventing the incandescent electric light bulb.

martial arts cultures call them *masters*. Western societies call them *mentors*. I call them *OGs* No matter the name used to describe them, it is important to understand their necessity in the quest to master your given passion.

In basketball, the influence and sharing of OGs happens mainly on two levels.

On the macro level, there are the superstars and icons who have influenced so many. Bill Russell, Larry Bird, Magic Johnson, Julius Erving, Diana Taurasi, Isiah Thomas, Michael Jordan, Tamika Catchings, Maya Moore, Lisa Leslie, Penny Hardaway, Candace Parker, Allen Iverson, Kobe Bryant, LeBron James, Stephen Curry... All those players had (and for some, are currently having) a massive influence on the generation coming after them. Millions grew up idolizing them and mimicking their moves. They played (or are currently playing) an integral part in producing the superstars we currently enjoy watching tearing down defenses.

Anthony Davis says Michael Jordan and LeBron James were his childhood heroes. Paul George idolized and mimicked Kobe Bryant growing up. Trae Young says his favorite player was Steve Nash, and states how much impact he had on his game. Steph Curry says that 5'3" NBA player Muggsy Bogues is the reason why he believed playing at the next level was possible despite being smaller than most growing up.

Those OGs are essential to inspire the youth and show them what can be possible. But it is the people who are here along the way, the OGs on the micro level, the everyday teachers of the game and life, who are the most important. A success story is built with so many people playing pivotal roles along the way. A parent, a dedicated coach, a school teacher, a physical trainer, an older friend, a brother or sister who believes in you, and more... Everyday-life OGs can come in many forms.

Jonathan Kazadi[11] is one of the best players to have ever come out of Switzerland. He credits his first coach, a local guy who loved the game and coached him from eight to thirteen years old, as the reason for his success.

NBA star and three time NBA Champion Draymond Green credits his college coach Tom Izzo for building him into the man and the player he is today. Many pros hold the same regards towards their high-school or college coaches.

Kevin Durant explained in tears that the real MVP was his mom, who was there each moment of the way, providing for him and doing all she could to help him pursue his dream. LeBron holds similar regards to his mom, who sacrificed so much to raise him with little means.

It is the people around you that will provide guidance through the ups and downs and will teach you valuable lessons about the game and life. Every good basketball player I've known has had one or several key people along the way who provided key support; helping them make a wise decision, stay out of trouble, gain a specific skill, or simply helped them believe.

---

[11] Jonathan Kazadi has been the starting point guard for Switzerland's National Team from 2010 up until now. He is considered one of the all-time best basketball players from Switzerland. He has played professionally in Switzerland, Spain, France and Germany.

On the flip side, having the wrong OG can be just as detrimental to your progress. I have met so many who had been ill-advised and regretted relying and trusting certain people.

It is your task to do your own research and recognize the people who will help you advance in the right direction. Beware, with all the marketing options that social media offers, it is becoming ever harder to see who is truly worth listening to and who is simply blowing smoke.

The right OGs will have an immense impact on your life. Recognize them.

Principle 7: Provoke The Lady

"There is a thing about luck...you don't know if it is good or bad until you have some perspective."

—ALICE HOFFMAN

Despite the amount of attractive attributes you possess, despite your experience, despite the quality of your choices, you will never secure her. No matter the amount of seduction you've got, it won't be enough to keep this lady by your side. Interpreting her signs is impossible. She will sometimes give you the hardest tests as a sign that she is riding with you. And other times, she will make it seem like she is your ride-or-die, until you realize she was actually cursing you from the start. She is the most uncontrollable, unpredictable, most beautiful one of all. We are all at her mercy and must accept her moods and work with her.

You may have guessed it... The Lady is what we commonly call "luck."

Any...and let me repeat it: ANY successful basketball journey (and any successful journey in general) is filled with the luck factor. Much more than anyone would admit.

One day at the beginning of the school year, close to my eighth birthday, a classmate whom I thought was cool bragged to the class about how he was starting basketball that same night. I came home that day asking my mom if I could start playing. If I am not mistaken, we showed up at practice the same day. My basketball journey started with luck.

Despite growing up in Switzerland, I was blessed that Coach T, a retired American professional player, settled in my town when I was around 12 years old. He had a son slightly younger than me, and his son was the reason why Coach T started coaching us in my local club when I was around 14. Thus, with pure luck I benefited from a great coach, an incredible motivator, and a true OG who gave us all the permission to dream.

Then there was my friendship with Paul and later Simon and Abdoul. Together we pushed ourselves every single day. We were on a similar mission, and Lady Luck made it so that our paths crossed. Who knows the number of hours I spent in a basketball gym with those three guys? And I loved each minute of training and going through this process with them. Had I been alone, had I not crossed paths with other guys as motivated and driven as I was, would I have spent that much time on my craft? Not a chance.

My final year of high school was hard. I was on the verge of failure. Failing meant repeating the year, which meant no more going to the United States to have a try at my dream. Following a silly argument with the coach, I simply left and never came back. I was teamless for over six months. It was ugly at the time, but it gave me the time I needed to focus on my schoolwork and get my grades back up. Sometimes, luck shows up in strange ways.

The following summer, I was called to try out with the under 20 years old national team. I was not a high-profile player, especially after being teamless for this long, and was a first-year player in a category that included a two-year group: 1989- and 1990-born players. From reliable sources, I knew that the coach wanted to cut me after training camp, but the assistant coach insisted on taking me. I was one of the last, if not *the* last, player selected. When the first official game arrived, everyone choked. I showed up. I kept showing up. I ended up being the top scorer of the team and second-best scorer in the whole FIBA European Championship that summer, with close to 20 points per game. How much did the role of luck play in this performance? A ton. This performance at the European Championships certainly put me on the map.

And luck did not stop there.... I was lucky to be born in a family that was financially stable and able to support me, allowed me to pursue my desire to play basketball, and put me in a situation to succeed by sending me to Worcester Academy for a year of prep school which gave me exceptional exposure and surrounded me with incredible people.

In Worcester, our top player got kicked out of school for bad behavior. Additionally, the Kevin Garnett-like stud brought over from the UK could never adjust to the US game. This meant a bigger role for me. I am the kind that shows up. I ended up being the second offensive option behind Billy Baron[12] (who would later represent Team USA and become a EuroLeague star).

Despite the incredible exposure and experience that playing at Worcester Academy offered me *(Michael Carter-Williams, Will Barton, Andre Drummond, Russ Smith, Ricky Ledo, and Nik Stauskas are a few future NBA players I competed against that year)*, the month of May (2010) arrived and I was optionless in terms of

---

[12] Billy Baron is a current EuroLeague player. He has played in Lithuania, Belgium, Spain, Turkey, Russia, and Serbia. He represented Team USA in the 2017 AmeriCup and won gold.

scholarship. Tony Bennett, head coach of The University of Virginia (ACC), where Billy Baron had signed, contacted his cousin, who was the third assistant coach at Florida Gulf Coast University, to tell him I was an absolute steal.

And that is how big of a role Lady Luck had to play for me to land an NCAA Division I scholarship offer.

I could go on and on about how lucky I have been throughout my basketball journey. But let me give you the other side of the coin:

Close to age 16, I started to feel pain in my groin. Diagnosis: pubalgia (or groin hernia).[13] This pain handicapped me for almost two years, including a six-month stretch where even walking was highly painful. Everyone thought my basketball days were gone.

When the pain got better, I logged long days in the gym and developed tendonitis in my left knee, which followed me for years. Throughout my college career, I could only jump off two feet, the pain being often too sharp to even do a standard layup.

The summer before leaving for Worcester Academy, I pulled my hamstring. Not knowing better, I played for months on pain medication (throughout the U20 national team campaign), followed by six weeks of strict rest and no rehabilitation. Three weeks into playing, I started to feel a sharp pain in my lower back. Since I did no rehab, my hamstring and glutes were so weak that all the pressure referred to my

---

[13] An injury in the pubis/adductors area caused by a disbalance of force between certain muscles.

spine. At 19 years old, I was the proud owner of a L5-S1 disc herniation. Did I stop? No, I played the whole season on it. Until this day, I still have no idea how I achieved this feat. It is probably the most impressive (but by far not the wisest) thing I have ever done.

Did coaches stop recruiting me after seeing me play? You bet. Already white, small, and not athletic—a combination that puts anyone hoping to earn a college scholarship at a huge disadvantage to start with—I was not able to bend down, make any sharp change of direction, or play any defense after the first quarter during the entire season. At least 10 NCAA Division I schools came to see the European shooter play at Worcester Academy. Most never talked to me again after that.

Then came the fact that the Swiss-to-US school grades conversion translated to a GPA below 2.0, making me ineligible and unable to receive a college scholarship. (Below a 2.0, you cannot even attend a formal university).

Did my options fly away? You bet. After much research, time wasted, missed scholarship opportunities, and an appeal, my GPA got bumped to a 2.01. At last, I was eligible and the dream stayed alive.

Again, I could go on and on about all the times Lady Luck dropped me hard throughout my career. But now is not the time for an autobiography.

I chose to give you examples of my journey and how luck influenced and shaped it, as my journey is the one I know about the most intimately. But I could tell you about the journey and path of any other former or current player, average or superstar, and the luck factor would be just as prominent.

Everything revolves around Lady Luck. The genes you were passed down, the education you receive, the cool classmate who makes you start playing the game, the coaches who cross your path, the parents who give you the freedom to choose your sport, the teammates who become your brothers or sisters and help you push through, the right play at the right time that makes you shine in front of the right people, and even the fact that this book is in your hands...

It is wise to be conscious and remind yourself to stay humble and appreciative when things are going well. On the flip side, when everything goes the wrong way, and it seems like the world has stopped spinning, keep up the spirit. The wheel turns.

Don't let positive events bring you too high and make you rest on your laurels; don't let negative ones bring you too low and make you quit on the dream. Give your maximum effort and love to the game. It is all you can do. Then let the lady choose.

Can Lady Luck be charmed in some way?

When I was at Worcester Academy and was receiving recruiting letters from different universities, I received a letter from Penn State University that ended up on my wall for many years. On the paper, a quote:

> *"I am a great believer in luck. And I find the harder I work, the more I have of it."*
>
> —THOMAS JEFFERSON

I, too, am a believer in luck. I believe it can be provoked. Are you? I'll let you decide and make your own choices.

I would like to share with you a story that has had a profound effect on me. It is a Taoist story[14] which reminds me that all I can do is to keep giving my best despite what luck, or life, brings my way:

There was an old farmer who had worked his crops for many years. One day the single horse he owned ran away. How would he keep working the farm without his horse? Upon hearing the news, his neighbors came to visit.

"Such bad luck, we are truly sorry," they said sympathetically.

"I don't know what is good or bad," the farmer replied.

The next morning the horse returned from the forest, bringing with it three other wild horses.

"How wonderful, you are now a rich man," the neighbors exclaimed.

"I don't know what is good or bad," replied the old man.

The following day, the farmer's son, while riding one of the untamed horses, was thrown and shattered his leg, making the stronger man of the family unable to work. The neighbors again came to offer their sympathy for what they called his "misfortune, and a tragedy."

"I don't know what is good or bad," answered the farmer again.

---

[14] Adapted by Dennis Adsit (https://www.newventureswest.com/real-lesson-taoist-farmer-story/)

The day after, military officials came to the village to draft young men into the army. A war had broken out and all young healthy men had to go fight and die for their country. But seeing that the son's leg was broken, they passed him by, and his life was saved. The neighbors congratulated the farmer on how well things had turned out.

"I don't know what is good or bad," said the farmer.

What seems to be bad luck today often proves to be great fortune tomorrow, and what seems like the luckiest thing today will at times prove to be the worst thing that could have happened. By giving your best, and focusing on the things you can control, you will come out a winner—no matter the outcome.

I would love to hear your encounter with lady luck. What event or situation that seemed like bad luck ended up being great fortune for you? Please do share it with me at basketballpath@gmail.com

Quarter Summary:

In this quarter, we went through seven principles that are of absolute necessity to understand and implement if you want to tap into your full basketball potential. These principles are the attitudes to adopt, the software to download and run in the background of your mind each day:

Principle 1: **Think Systems**

Systems give you a clear route to follow, stride after stride, to bridge the gap between your current and desired state of being (or playing).

Principle 2: **Understand Your Profile**

Understanding your attributes will help you know which direction to take in your training. Your profile should dictate your work, not the other way around.

Principle 3: **Give Love and Passion**

Having a deep love for the game is essential and is what will make you push through the inevitable obstacles along the way. Without love and passion for the game, you won't have what it takes to reach your full potential.

Principle 4: **Make 'Em Count**

The rep you took at practice on Friday night might end up being the one that makes you good enough to hit the game-winner a week later! Take responsibility for each rep and each minute on the floor. They all count.

Principle 5: **Visualize**

The brain does not see a difference between real action and internal visualization. Use it to perfect your game and skills. Start your journey using our guided meditations at www.strideyourpassion.com/services.

Principle 6: **Recognize the OGs**

Guidance is key in any sports career. Recognize and surround yourself with the right teachers of the game *and life*.

Principle 7: **Provoke The Lady**

Luck is part of the process. Provoke it and embrace what comes your way.

Don't worry, I will not leave you here. All these principles will be included in your personal MyStride system that we will build together in the Fourth Quarter.

We will now look into the three pillars on which the approach is built on. Understanding them will be the first step to building your individualized system.

PLAY WITHIN THE SYSTEM

"The whole is greater than the sum of its parts."

—Aristotle

As discussed in Principle 1, it is essential to think in terms of systems. In fact, the whole purpose of this book is to help you implement the MyStride system in your basketball (and life) journey. Systems allow you to channel knowledge and apply, moment by moment, the necessary actions and behaviors to get you to a desired destination.

A system, like a machine, is built with different parts. It is important to thoroughly understand each one of them along with their purpose. Only when they are understood and applied simultaneously can the results be fruitful.

In this Second Quarter, we will explore in detail each one of the three parts, or pillars the MyStride Approach is built upon. With the understanding of each part, we will see how they can interact together and multiply results.

By the end of this quarter, you will have gained all the necessary tools and knowledge to not only follow the guided self-implementation from the Fourth Quarter, but also create a personal, tailored system that will impact your game and your life in many ways.

Pillar I: Know Thyself

*"Know thyself, know thy enemy. A thousand battles,
a thousand victories."*

—Sun Tzu

A team needs a lot of parts to be complete and successful. And I believe that anyone, no matter their size, shape, or form, can find ways to be valuable. By having a deep sense of understanding of yourself and your surroundings, you can become a worthy piece within your team.

Let's look into the above quote, from the ancient Chinese war general and strategist Sun Tzu[15]. "Know thyself, know thy enemy. A thousand battles, a thousand victories."

We can deduce from it that there are two parts of knowledge to focus on :

Know thyself. Purely on an individual standpoint, knowing the self is about being aware of your profile as a basketball player—your own body, your own movements, and your own individual skill set—as explained in Principle 2 from the First Quarter. This knowledge helps you be realistic, identify your strengths and your weaknesses, and be conscious of the things you can rely on—as well as the ones you cannot.

Know thy enemy. This second part is trickier to put into context. As I interpret the quote, what is meant by "enemy" is

---

[15] Sun Tzu was a Chinese general, military strategist, writer, and philosopher who lived in ancient China (around 500 BC). Sun Tzu is credited as the author of the book *The Art of War.*

anything external that can affect you. Understanding your environment will allow you to always place yourself in an optimal position to make external factors your allies rather than your enemies. In basketball, the main external factors that can impact your game are your coaches and their style of play, your teammates, and—on game day only—your actual enemy: your opponent.

Gaining such knowledge takes time, effort and a great deal of self-reflexion. It also requires being as objective as possible, which is not easy. To help you out, I want to share with you a few useful strategies to learn more about "thyself" and about "thy enemy".

Learning About "Thyself"

WATCH FILM. And be hard on yourself. Men lie, women lie, film doesn't. Watch game films, record your shooting series and your one-on-one games. Film reveals everything. A dip in your shot that makes it slower, all the box-outs you missed, an open teammate you did not pass the ball to, a move that has no impact—anything you want and need to know is on film.

TALK TO YOURSELF. Each rep counts. Let me say it again: each rep counts. This is what we talked about in the fourth principle of the First Quarter, and is the foundation of the compound effect (more on this later).

Get into the habit of correcting yourself on every rep you take and every move you make. Don't be shy; talk out loud. This practice will help you become aware of what you are doing and raise your consciousness.

If you do something very nice, reward yourself: "Nicely done, (insert your name), the execution speed was great." When something is not well done, give yourself some encouragement and make sure you tell yourself how to correct the small details on the next rep: "Chin the ball (insert your name)"— *when you go to the layup to protect it.*

The women's basketball team at Florida Gulf Coast University is one of the most successful Division I teams in America. From 2009–10 through 2021-22, the team had a combined 368-64 record. Each year, they beat schools from the Big Five conferences. During the 2019–20 season alone, they beat the likes of Duke, Notre Dame (the 2018 national champion), South Florida, and Temple University. For a small Division I school, this is beyond belief.

The mastermind behind this? Coach Karl Smesko. During my years at FGCU, I have watched freshmen arriving at the program as under-recruited players and being transformed into all-conference contenders in a matter of two seasons. Coach Smesko's number one rule: each player has to verbally comment on each shot they take at practice. He instructs his players to say "back half" whenever they miss short, "straighter" when the ball would go left or right, and "good miss" when the ball goes long. When the ball falls right in the net, they would say "arrows." The team has been number one in the country in three-pointers made year in and year out. In 2020–21, they drained 11.8 threes per game, 1.4 more than any other Division I team. Coincidence?

LOOK ABOVE. If you are serious about your stuff and train accordingly, you will get better. This is a dangerous moment.

Some young players suddenly get ahead of themselves when performing well, believing they are special turf.

If you are the most valuable player on your team, then look at the best player in your city. After you become number one in the city, check if someone is better than you in your area and chase him. Are you already the best in your area? Then what about your country?

There will always be players to look up to and learn from. Focus on them rather than the ones below you in terms of level. This will help you stay humble and always continue improving.

The more you know about yourself, your game, your abilities, and your shortcomings, the smarter you can work and the better you will become.

Learning About "Thy Enemy"

As I stated earlier, "the enemy" is not referring to people trying to take you down. It is a metaphor for your surroundings: anything that lies outside of the self can have a positive or negative impact on you. Understanding and thoroughly knowing about it is therefore of utmost importance.

I assume that everyone agrees that the ultimate goal of practice—individual and team—is to maximize performance on the court during official competitions. Yes, training is fun by itself, and this should never be forgotten, but the aim of it is to perform in 5 vs. 5 or 3 vs. 3, whatever your style.

When competition comes, who decides if you will be on the floor? Who decides the plays? Who decides on the responsibilities you can undertake within the game? And who decides if you will receive the ball or not? It is your coaches and your teammates!

YOUR COACH. The coach has a lot of responsibilities and power within a team. His influence on the players and on the game goes much beyond simply choosing who is on the floor. Let me tell you a valuable insight that young (and older) players often forget: your coach, no matter where you are in the world, is human. He has emotions, he has affinities, he has opinions, and he has his own perception of reality.

So ultimately, playing time and responsibilities on the floor are easier to get when the coach wants you to have them rather than when he does not. They are not necessarily given to the best player, nor the hardest worker or the kindest teammate. This is something very hard to grasp for most players. As players, we always think that fairness is the only thing that comes into play. It is not. Let me illustrate with an example.

When I was young, there was a player in my city who, in my opinion, was the best point guard in the whole country at the time. He was more athletic than most, very skilled, a fierce competitor, and relentless on defense. Throughout the year, he was consistently the best performer with the city selection team, and his club team was top-ranked in the region. But that guy was not even considered to be part of the U18 national team. As a matter of fact, he did not even get invited to tryouts while players much inferior to him, including myself, were given this opportunity. Why? Because the national team head coach did not like the player's attitude on the court (walking with a chip on his shoulder) and because he thought his style of play would not fit his system. He ended up selecting two pass-first point guards while the best point guard in the country did not even have the chance to prove himself.

Was it right? I don't believe so. Is this how it works always, everywhere? This example is extreme, but things like this happen very often.

As a player, you need to be adaptable and tuned into the expectations of the coach because he alone decides on your playing time. Only on the floor can you compete, get buckets, get better, and get noticed. **Your job is therefore to become an expert at executing what is expected of you on the floor.**

> Does your coach like players who talk on defense? *Then scream on defense!*

> Does he like guys who take charges? *Attempt charges until you bleed!*

> Does he ask you to find a man to box out each time a shot goes up? *Put your body on someone each time the ball goes up!*

> Does he want players who dive on the floor for loose balls? *Practice your floor dives when no one is watching to avoid skin burns, then start flying all over.*

The more you will do what your coach expects and wants to see, the more trust and playing time you will enjoy. The more trust and playing time you get, the more confidence you gain. The more confidence you have, the more you can try new things and take responsibilities with no fear of failure and, as a result, make progress. It is a self-perpetuating cycle.

Try going 1 vs. 1 coast-to-coast after having taken three charges in one quarter and see if your coach pulls you out. Try to take a long-range three-pointer after giving the most energy on defense and lifting your whole team up, and see if you end up on the bench. Try to do anything you want after nullifying the other team's best rebounder by boxing him out every time, and let's see if someone will come from the bench to take your spot on the floor.

It won't happen.

When I was a freshman in college, I was desperate to find a way to be on the floor. I was surrounded by good players who had, for the most part, more experience than me and were taller, faster and jumped higher than I did. On top of it all, the player at my position was the best on the team and a local star. Getting on the floor would not be a walk in the park.

I quickly realized how much my coach loved it when his players took charges. This was his own definition of toughness. At practice, when someone took a charge, he would clap his hands and walk the other way screaming, "ChaaAAARRGE."

Say no more, Coach.

I began to take charges. I took every opportunity I could. The coach would often give advice on how to take more charges, and I applied them. And he loved it. When the season came around, I was able to enjoy higher than expected playing time.

I was at the time not good enough to justify so much trust, but the fact that my coach knew that I would do whatever he asked and expected on the floor was enough for him to give me this opportunity.

Other players were better and more suited to be on the floor, but they wanted to do it their own way. They did it their own way on the bench. I started the year with a miserable percentage from the field, but thanks to the other things I was doing on the floor, I did not have to fear for my playing time and was able to slowly build up confidence. After an adjustment period, I started to hit more shots, and ended up having a great year, making the Atlantic Sun Conference All-Freshman team and being a contender for the Freshman of the Year award.

Your coach can be your enemy or your ally. Make him an ally by always being in tune with what he expects from you. Be his best, most reliable soldier.

YOUR TEAMMATES. Your teammates are the ones playing with you and passing you the ball. Getting angry at your teammates when they make mistakes, acting selfish on the court, holding a negative attitude toward the team—all those things will have a negative effect on your game.

When I was a sophomore in college, a new point guard arrived on the team. His name was Brett Comer. That player, I am not exaggerating, was unbelievably talented. He had the type of talent and feel for the game that you rarely come across in a lifetime. He was doing things that no one can teach. It seemed like he had eyes in the back of his head. Brett quickly became our floor general and gained a lot of responsibilities. Unfortunately, he and I were of total opposite character. As opposite as anyone can be.

Instead of accepting and understanding our differences, we clashed, and although we had mutual respect for one another, we did not get along very well. As a result, an impact could be felt on the floor and I believe we both suffered from it. I lost playing time because I wasn't able to keep my cool, and he was clearly the better and more valuable player for the team. On the flip side his creative options were reduced as his best shooter was glued to the bench.

Everyone lost in this situation—him, me, the team, and the coaches.

Brett Comer finished his career as a top 25 all-time leader in assists in the history of the NCAA. How I wish he would have pursued a professional career. He would have been incredible in the European style of play. Instead, he chose to coach. He is now coaching at the highest levels.

It is of high importance and within the ability of every player to spend a fair amount of energy to understand themselves and their surroundings. Being aware, understanding, and applying this knowledge will help you develop as a player, enjoy better roles, and earn more freedom on the court.

There are, however, certain things that a player should never do, no matter how much he wants to enjoy playing time. Here is "the code of the *do nots*" to gain playing time:

1. Never snitch on teammates to make them look bad in front of the coach or anyone who could have influence

directly or indirectly (unless an integrity or life-threatening situation is at play).

2. Never engage in anything that goes against your integrity as a person for any reason, not even for precious floor time.

3. Never try to be Mr. Nice Guy or fake being someone you are not to please others.

Pillar II: Seek Guidance

*"True guidance is like a small torch in a dark forest.
It doesn't show everything once. But gives enough light
for the next step to be safe."*

—SWAMI VIVEKANANDA

The second pillar of the MyStride Approach is guidance. Guidance, in any area of life, is of utmost importance.

As stated in the sixth principle of the First Quarter, *Recognize the OGs*, there are very few to no one out there who have figured it out alone. Every successful person in any field has had people who guided, supported, inspired, pushed, and mentored them to defy their limits and reach the next level.

Benjamin Bloom[16], pioneer in the field of talent development and Anders K. Ericsson[17], an internationally recognized human performance expert both stress the importance of having a quality mentor in the quest for excellence.

Ericsson states that the making of an expert is facilitated by two factors. Firstly, the ability of the person to constantly and deliberately push towards the zone of discomfort to expand knowledge and skills, a notion he calls "deliberate practice" (explained with image 4 from the fourth principle in the First

---

[16] Benjamin Bloom (1913-1999) was an educational psychologist. He is well known for his contributions in attaining mastery, and for creating the Bloom's Taxonomy.

[17] K. Anders Erikson (1947-2020) was an internationally recognized psychologist who studied the psychological nature of expertise and human performance.

Quarter). Secondly, the presence of an expert in the field in question who can guide the person throughout the journey.

The power and importance of guidance and mentorship is not a secret. Universities have programs to help guide their students and accelerate learning. The world's largest corporations spend millions to form their future leaders. Team sport coaches love to have older players on their roster to lead the younger ones with their experience...

For young players with hoop dreams, basketball is the most important thing in the world. Unfortunately, the vast majority of them either do not have the privilege of receiving good guidance, fail to recognize its necessity, or simply reject it when it is available. I have seen so many players refuse help and advice, wanting to do it alone because they thought they knew better.

Ironically, the very elites, the ones who would logically need less guidance and support to perform, are often those who value it the most. NBA players trust skills, athletics and mental coaches to help them reach their full potential. If the best in the world seek guidance to perform better, I believe young players should take the subject seriously and be open to receive advice.

Guidance is at the core of the MyStride Mentorship program we offer our clients. Working with a knowledgeable mentor will save you energy, help you gain knowledge faster, increase motivation, and avoid pitfalls you wouldn't see alone.

Recognize the OGs. Those who know what hard work really is, what it is like to be in your shoes, in your head and who can help you get closer to your fullest potential. OGs who truly understand your love.

Pillar III: Track and Know

"If you cannot measure it, you cannot improve it."

—PETER DUCKER

Each year, as summer vacation approached, I could not wait to dedicate my days to basketball. I knew what I needed to work on which led me to construct an elaborate plan to improve my game. I could visualize myself going through the process, and being a much more complete player by the beginning of the following season. Ball handling, working on my skinny and fragile body, and bettering pick-and-roll knowledge was of utmost importance for me to take my game to the next level. It was all in my summer plan. Every day, I would follow this routine to elevate my game...

A few months later, when September and team practices approached, I'd realize I did not follow the regimen I had genuinely set for myself. I was no closer to what I had envisioned to become. I had done nothing but shooting, playing one-on-one and pickup games all summer.

I wasn't the only victim of this pattern. Over the years, I have witnessed many of my motivated teammates and basketball friends adopt a similar behavior when it comes to summer vacation. I can vividly remember my Croatian roommate and great friend Filip, a 6'9" (205 cm) small forward who had an unbelievable touch and amazing mobility for his size (but not so unbelievable work ethic), leaving campus in May, telling us he would train like hell and come back playing like Kevin Durant... Did not happen.

The pattern goes as follows: excited and hopeful about the development time or new beginnings, making promises to follow a thorough plan to reach new heights, not following the plan, and waking up a few months later short of expectations. You may recognize yourself in this behavior.

Throughout my basketball career, rare were the periods during which I was able to sustain the consistency in the areas I wanted and needed for myself to grow as a player. This pattern hurt me greatly in the long term. The problem was never work ethic, discipline, or ignorance. I would simply always find myself weeks and months down the road realizing I had forgotten about my plans.

One summer, I accidentally stumbled on a solution.

As usual, I had made great plans. I was even more motivated, fresh off a trip to the NCAA March Madness Sweet 16 round. But a few weeks before the summer began, my knee tendonitis flared up, and to my dismay, I was not able to train during the full break. Since I could not play, but was eager to find a way to improve, I made a funny bet with myself: I would make 30,000 floaters during that off-season. I had about 10 weeks.

I was always notoriously bad when it came to the game around the basket, especially floaters. It was a big weakness of mine. I remember a game against The University of Miami, going past Shane Larkin[18], arriving in the paint, and launching a floater. *Launching* is the right word. The ball left my hand, went straight against the backboard, and bounced off

---

[18] Shane Larkin played college ball at the University of Miami, and has been playing professionally in the NBA and Euro League.

of it. It never even got close to touching the rim. I had just thrown a mega brick, standing less than two meters away from the basket.

That summer, I divided the amount of shots I needed to make on a daily basis to get to my goal of 30,000. It was slightly more than 400 per day. Then I defined a few different types of floaters I would work on: left hand, right hand, two-feet left hand, two-feet right hand, etc.... I bought one of these plastic tubes that you hook on the rim, rolling the ball back to you when you score, and I was set. Every day, I would stand beside the basket, would shoot rounds of 50 made shots at slow speed for each type of floater I wanted to work on until it added up to around 400 makes. I would then write down my numbers in a column next to the date on a piece of paper.

This was a revelation. I'd know exactly what had been accomplished on each workout and where this workout stood in the big picture. I could leave the gym satisfied with myself, not wondering if what I had done was enough.

Image 4: Sophomore year. Going by Shane Larkin, thanks to the help of a screen from a teammate, on the way to throwing up a brick from inside the paint.

Without knowing it at the time, I had applied a sort of reverse engineering process: I had started with a final outcome I had full control over, and broke it down to the small strides that needed to be taken to get there. It gave me a clear picture of the moment-to-moment output needed. By applying the small steps, I knew I was on the path to attaining my desired outcome.

I had stumbled on something immensely powerful that no one had ever taught me in school or at basketball: **tracking**. Tracking gave me direction and helped me stay accountable and consistent over time.

The real magic happened a few months later during practice with my new team at Chaminade University of Honolulu (I transferred to an NCAA Division II school in Hawaii my senior season). As I drove to the basket and made a bad decision, the coach stopped the play and came to me. He said something along these lines: "Christophe, why do you make your life harder? Just shoot one of those floaters you are so good at. You have such a good percentage."

The coach did not know, but this comment created an explosion in my chest. I had spent the past two and a half years inconsistently trying to improve my finishes around the basket, taking risks at practice and games, being benched, seeing my coaches at FGCU (rightfully) rolling their eyes when seeing me trying to finish close to the basket. I was now at Chaminade University and shots around the basket were part of my strengths. It took a simple reverse engineering and a tracking method—and a knee injury—to turn this area of my game from weakness to strength.

How I wish I could tell you that from then on, I started tracking daily actions for consistency purposes, and I was able to follow through....

Unfortunately, I can't. I failed to recognize the power of this practice due to a lack of awareness (or by lack of guidance at the time). It was not until five years later, when my basketball career had already ended, that I was reintroduced to it thanks to my co-worker Stefan, whom I mentioned in the introduction of the book.

Measuring and tracking is like constantly facing a mirror. **It allows you to see exactly who you are and therefore elevates the consciousness about what you do and why you do it.** It helps you execute the small everyday steps that may seem insignificant, but add up over time.

The practice of tracking your actions will allow you to:

- Greatly improve your consistency.
- Know if you act accordingly to what you want and need to do.
- Develop rock-solid habits.
- Increase consciousness and self-accountability.
- Get constant reminders about your actions.
- Help you take a stride forward each day.
- Stop lying to yourself about what you are actually doing.
- Impact your confidence positively.

Let me elaborate on the last (very important) point of this list: *How can tracking influence confidence?*

Gary Mack gives a great definition of confidence in his book *Mind Gym*[19] : "Confidence is the emotional knowing that you are prepared, mind, body, and spirit, for anything."

By establishing a process you truly believe in and following it consistently with a proven track record, you will automatically fall into the mental state Gary Mack describes.

The key lies in the rightful identification of the actions you must perform over time... Their constant implementation will lead to the Eighth Wonder of the World.

---

[19] Mack, Gary, and David Casstevens. Mind Gym an Athlete's Guide to Inner Excellence. New York u.a.: McGraw-Hill, 2007.

The Eighth Wonder:
The Compound Effect

"Success doesn't come from doing extraordinarily difficult things. It's doing simple things, consistently."

—UNKNOWN

The world has hosted incredible men and women, whose intelligence and intensity brought decisive advances for mankind. One of them was Albert Einstein. Einstein, known for his brilliance and multiple groundbreaking science achievements, once declared: "Compound interest is the Eighth Wonder of the World. He who understands it earns it; he who does not pays it."

I am not remotely close to considering myself a bright mind, but I believe I am somewhat clever. If one of the brightest humans to ever walk the face of the earth offered such praise about something—*compound interest*—ranking it as a Wonder of the World, I believe it is worth spending some time looking into it.

The compound interest Einstein is talking about is essentially a financial term. The *compound effect* is when the same principle is adapted to life instead of strictly finances. The compound effect is everywhere. It is a principle of great fascination to me. I would write a book about it, but there is already a bestseller out there called *The Compound Effect*[20].

To better understand it, we will first look into the financial term with numbers and then see how this phenomenon is adaptable to basketball and other things we do...or don't do.

---

[20] Hardy, Darren. *The Compound Effect: Multiplying Your Success, One Simple Step at a Time.*

Back in the day, if you placed your money in a bank, you would receive a good interest rate on your investment. In other words, the bank would pay you a percentage in return for lending them your money. (Today, banks offer close to no interest, and this is why the stock market has gained in popularity despite being more risky). For the sake of the example, let's pretend we are back in the golden age when banks would offer great interest returns.

There are different ways to receive interest. Let's focus on two of them: simple and compounded.

In both scenarios, we will start our investment with a principal (the money you invest) of $1,000 and a yearly interest rate of 10% (the percentage of the principal you receive in return).

SCENARIO 1: Simple interest annually. It means that we will receive 10% of our principal each year, but the interest will be calculated solely on the initial principal.

1. Simple interest:

  - Year 1: 1,000 x 0.10 = 100
  - Year 2: 1,000 x 0.10 = 100
  - Year 3: 1,000 x 0.10 = 100
  - Year 4: 1,000 x 0.10 = 100
  - Year 5: 1,000 x 0.10 = 100

Total value of the investment at the end of year 5:
1,000 + 100 (year 1) + 100 (year 2) + 100 +100 + 100 = $ **1,500**

SCENARIO 2: Compounded interest annually. It means that the earned interest of each year is included in the calculation of the following year's interest. The interest will therefore be 10% of the principal plus all previously earned interests.

2. Compounded interest:

- Year 1: 1,000 x 0.10 = 100
- Year 2: 1,100 x 0.10 = 110
- Year 3: 1,210 x 0.10 = 121
- Year 4: 1,331 x 0.10 = 133.1
- Year 5: 1,464.1 x 0.10 = 146.4

Total sum at the end of year 5:

1,000 + 100 + 110 + 121 + 133.1 + 146.4 = $ **1,610.5**

As you see, the compounded interest method creates bigger gains every year. In the short run, this difference is minimal. However, if we give more time to both situations above, let's say 20 years, the results speak for themselves:

$1,000 on 10% simple interest annually for 20 years = $3,000

$1,000 on 10% compounded interest annually for 20 years = $6,728

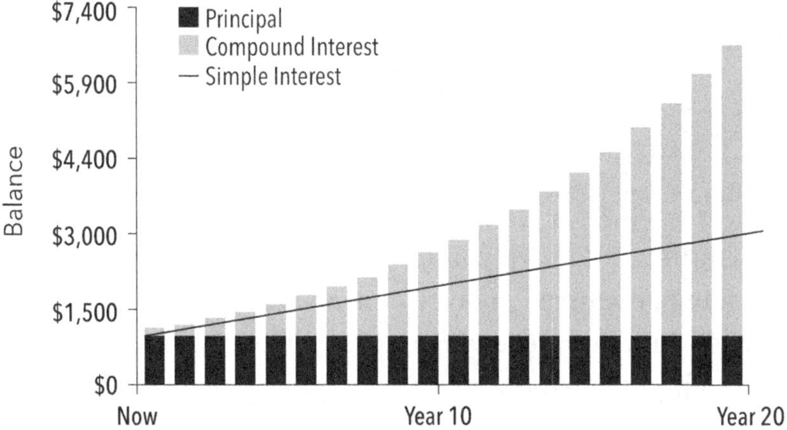

Image 5: $1000 on 10% compounded interest vs. simple interest over 20 years.

The more time you give the compound interest to work, the more your gains add up. It follows an exponential curve. Great, so what do these money-related problems have to do with basketball?

Everything!

In the same way the compound interest works with money, the compound effect works with your basketball skills and knowledge.

When we make small gains in any area of life, and use those small gains to create more gains, progress happens exponentially over time just like shown in *image 5*. As stated in the book of the same name, **the compound effect is the principle of reaping huge rewards from a series of small choices over time**. To tap into the compound effect, you must use the small progress made during each practice session—*in the form of new skills, knowledge or experience*—and incrementally build on them over and over and over, *as explored in the fourth principle from the First Quarter, Make'em Count.*

The aim of using and applying the MyStride Approach is to use the compound effect to your full advantage and benefit from making exponential progress over time:

By training effectively and efficiently with a deep understanding of yourself and your environment (Pillar I), setting proper direction, receiving the right advice, and mentoring through guidance (Pillar II), you will increase the **quality** of your practices and get more out of them. By establishing a tailored system through reverse engineering and proper tracking (Pillar III), you will achieve great **consistency**. Put together, **quality and consistency** will compound over time to something great.

The Inverse Curve

You have probably heard the following quote before:

"Sometimes you have to get worse before you get better."
—TOM WATSON

Anyone deciding to work toward reaching their full potential and really strive for perfection will have to go through periods during which they are worse off and during which performance will suffer. The pursuit of excellence exposes weaknesses and flaws. It makes one operate in zones of discomfort and unknown territory.

The graphic below shows the progression curve of a player looking for long-term development, compared to a player worried about instant results and relying on acquired skills.

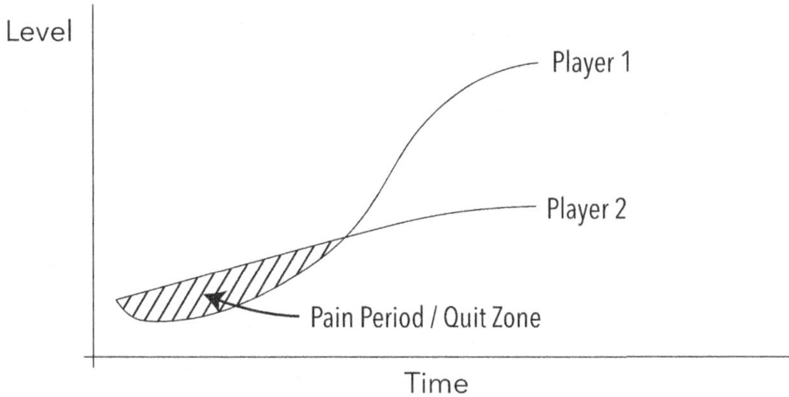

Image 6: The inverse curve.

Starting at the same level, Player 1 sees the big picture. He does not judge himself by his current results, but rather by how far out of his comfort zone he puts himself and how conscious he is of applying the proper movements and concepts. With this mindset, the focus is put on understanding and acquiring a broad base of skills and knowledge to build on, leaving the immediate results on the back seat.

Player 2 is focused on getting results right now. He is good enough to play at the level he currently plays at and judges himself on how many baskets he can score and how effective he is on the court, right now. This attitude forces him to stay within his comfort zone. He relies on what works now and rarely tries new movements. Initially, he certainly scores more and gets better results than Player 1 does, but he develops with gaps and flaws in his game.

After having passed the pain period (or quit zone), during which performance can be strongly affected, Player 1 notices that, thanks to his groundwork, every additional skill and technique gets integrated faster and faster. He is building on the interest gained. His progress curve steepens. Before long, Player 1 passes Player 2 whose progress curve is slow, linear and stalling due to having focused on instant results and failing to gain a wide range of skills and proper fundamentals to build on.

Stephen Curry spent one full summer changing his shot when he was in high school. Steph used to shoot with a very low release, and he realized that he would not be able to play at the next level unless his release was higher. He spent the whole summer between his sophomore and junior year of high school working on releasing the ball from a higher point. In multiple interviews, he called this time the most frustrating summer of his life.

Before undergoing this change, he was already the best and most accurate shooter wherever he went. But he had enough consciousness and self-criticism to realize his shooting form, although efficient in high school, would not translate at the college level against better and taller athletes. Changing his shot initially resulted in more misses, as if his game was taking a step back... I don't believe I need to tell you what happened next.

In 1997, at age twenty-two, Tiger Woods was the No. 1 ranked golfer in the world. After winning a major golf championship, Woods decided to change his swing. People thought he had lost his mind. But he knew that his swing had a small defect, affecting accuracy and exposing his body to injuries, which would hurt him in the long run. For two years, Tiger went back to the basics and reconstructed his swing with a swing coach. For two years, he did not win one major golf tournament. But as soon as he mastered his new movement, he enjoyed unprecedented domination in the world of golf. From 1999 to 2002, Tiger won 35% of the PGA Tour events and 44% of the majors he competed in.

Guys like Stephen Curry and Tiger Woods were already world class at their craft before making big changes in their games. They chose poorer results in the present to reap bigger rewards down the road. If those guys are ready to take a step back and get worse for a while before enjoying even greater success, I believe we should all consider this process ourselves.

Every single dribble, every single shot, every pass, and all defensive possessions are opportunities to grow as a player and gain skills, knowledge and experience. They should therefore be treated with utmost importance—every single day. Yes, your performances may suffer temporarily when making necessary adjustments. You must be willing to get worse before you can ride the exponential curve of progress and improve faster. This is an interesting paradox in sports and in life.

Life is a matter of small choices, small actions, small sacrifices, made daily over a long period of time. As good old Albert Einstein said: "He who understands it, earns it; he who does not, pays it."

Quarter Summary:

The MyStride Approach is a simple combination of the 3 pillars we just explored. When applied in concert, over time, progress compounds into great results as each action and each moment is used towards a definite aim.

Pillar I: **Know Thyself.**

Become an expert at knowing and understanding yourself and your surroundings. Be your own hardest critic and as detail-oriented as possible. Take time to analyze what your coach wants from you and how to interact with your teammates. This knowledge will help you understand what to work on and how to increase your value as a player and as a teammate.

Pilar II: **Seek Guidance.**

Benefit from the presence of a seasoned, highly experienced individual to guide you and support you along your path. Be open to feedback and apply lessons learned. True experience is irreplaceable.

Pillar III: **Track and Know.**

Measuring and tracking is like constantly facing a mirror. It allows you to see exactly who you are on top of elevating your consciousness about the things you do and why you do them. It constantly reminds you of the small daily steps that will make a difference in the long run, and it helps catch and correct wrong steps in a timely manner.

The Eighth Wonder: **The Compound Effect.**

Each action you perform works either for or against you. By applying the three pillars of the MyStride Approach, you will make the Eighth Wonder of the World work in your favor. Understand it, and earn it.

Image 7: The three pillars of the MyStride Approach lead to compounding results.

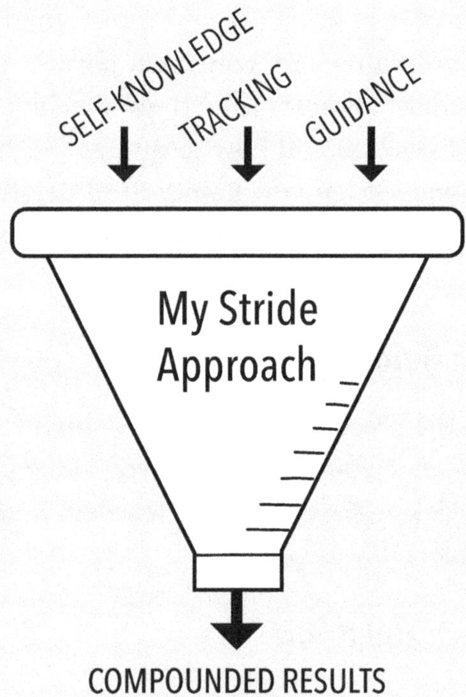

STAY IN THE GAME

"Some [athletes] have a belief system that says failure is a shameful thing. In truth, life is based upon failures. If you don't fail, you're probably not challenging yourself enough."
—Gary Mack, Mind Gym

Failure is a "non-negotiable". It will happen. Hurdles and pitfalls will stand in your way and make you face failure no matter what you pursue in life. That being said, to fail really hurts, and really sucks. So much so that players get into all sorts of emotional states, often falling off track when facing rough times. More than one "would be" great player quit too early or got lost going through the inevitable roadblocks on the way. The good news is that in basketball, and in sports in general, obstacles are often quite similar, identifiable, and predictable.

In this quarter, we will go through the five most common hurdles that lead to fatal failures for basketball players who dream big. Knowing what is coming ahead is of paramount importance to either avoid it or be prepared when it comes.

Awareness is key. It will be your job to put in the necessary work to analyze your circumstances and identify if you are headed straight into a wall, or if you are unconsciously stuck in a pitfall.

Hercules had to perform 12 labors to free himself and achieve immortality. You will have to identify and overcome specific roadblocks to unlock your full potential and follow a magical basketball journey. Since identifying and overcoming them will require some serious, continuous work, we will also call them labors.

Labor I: Overcome the Current

*"Whenever you find yourself on the side of the majority,
it is time to pause and reflect."*

—Mark Twain

Let's look into a couple of social dynamic facts.

FACT #1: All of us are influenced by the people we surround ourselves with. No matter who you are or where you come from, it is happening. Jim Rohn, a famous American entrepreneur and author, says that we are the average of the five people we spend the most time with. He is spot on.

FACT #2: Most careers do not require one to put in much effort until he or she actually enters the work world. Many go through life without much of a purpose until they find a path. They usually seek comfort, entertainment, and acceptance until they find it.

The net result of these two facts is something I call the *current*. It's fun, it's chill, it's tempting. And mostly, it offers some cool stuff: parties, girls and boys, social media, Netflix watching, fashion... This current is created because, according to fact #2, most young people end up seeking acceptance and instant gratification by conforming to what others do. As a result, fact #1 is activated, creating a herd of people with shared habits and thoughts by simple association.

In sports, a career is short-lived and so much more competitive early on. People wishing for it must therefore start taking things seriously much earlier. To do and achieve special things, special action must be taken. Machiavelli[21] said it best with his famous quote from *The Prince*: "The end justifies the means."

Following the current to be "normal" is therefore not the best path to stand out. If you are on the journey to become the best basketball player you can be (or excel in any other given field and really stand out), acting like everyone else will most likely not produce the results you are hoping for. For extraordinary results, extraordinary actions must be taken.

Understanding these social dynamic facts makes it easier to bend them and use them to your advantage in your quest to fulfill your ambitions.

How to use fact #1 to your advantage:

Dedicate your time to people who help you get closer to your desired place. Call it selfish? I don't agree. I am not telling you to use people for your own benefits without giving anything in return. Instead, I am saying to be selective with your time and give it to the ones who will make you better. An inspiring friend, the guy in your area who trains like hell, the person who has more discipline than you—all of these are checks. By surrounding yourself with the right people, their positive traits will rub off on you.

How to use fact #2 to your advantage:

Have you ever seen or heard of anyone achieving something special by doing the same things most are doing? Me neither.

---

[21] Nicolò Machiavelli (1469-1527) was an Italian statesman who lived during the Renaissance. He is best known for his political treatise *The Prince*.

If you are caring for the same things, training the same way, and taking the same actions most are, you are in it. Meaning: you are going in the wrong direction.

Weird, obsessive, crazy, and *idiot* are all words you will hear on your path if you are dedicated enough. People don't like to see others strive for something, especially when they themselves are scared of being judged.

I definitely faced these critics—from friends, from school teachers, and even from my own family. If you are in the same situation, I would like to tell you that you aren't weird. You are simply a passionate person following your heart and daring to dream big. Those going against the current are often the ones who will end up being creative and will achieve at least part of their dreams. They are the ones living their own truth. If you feel comfortable with your basketball in hand while all your friends are chatting with girls or boys, scrolling through social media, going out late at night, playing video games, or doing whatever else, it is completely normal and okay. You need not be like them or anyone. You need to be you. Most peoples' paths are not basketball. Yours is.

But beware: facing the current is not easy and often brings its fair share of difficulties. Many will stand in the short term, but most will fold in the long run. The strongest ones are not necessarily the ones who make it the farthest. The luckiest ones are. The ones who, by luck, see a ray of light that gives them the energy to keep going: an OG, a book (this book), access to a basketball gym, a close friend on the same journey, or simply the right action at the right time. Lady Luck comes in many forms.

As long as you follow the three rules below, I believe it is safe and even recommended to go for what is inside you.

1. **RADIATE POSITIVE VIBES.** Being angry, unkind, mean, or inconsiderate will never make you a better player. I made this mistake a thousand times over and paid a high price for it. I am still paying my debt.

2. **TAKE CARE OF YOUR SCHOOL GRADES.** We are living within a system—political, educational, cultural—and school is at the heart of it. Whether it is fair or not, many jobs you will one day either want, need, or have to fall back on out of necessity require school certifications. Neglect school and it will be the equivalent of Dwayne "The Rock" Johnson punching you in the face before a date. Your chances of success, no matter how you define it, will be much lower.

3. **DRUGS, CIGARETTES, AND ALCOHOL ARE BAD.** Stay away from them! They have a much larger effect on you and your performance than you might think, no matter how old you are. Not only can they have a detrimental effect on your body and mind, but they each carry with them a significant addiction risk—which could ruin your life and those of your loved ones. Want to be *really cool*? Learn to go to parties and interact with people without using any substances. Or even better, work on your game while others are at parties.

Labor II: Compare Functionally

"While you're out there partying, horsing around, someone out there at the same time is working hard. Someone is getting smarter and someone is winning. Just remember that."

—Arnold Schwarzenegger

An incredible amount of our life—decisions, attitudes, and beliefs—are shaped by the people we hang around with (remember fact #1 of Labor I). As a direct extension, being around people automatically triggers comparison. Whether we like it or not, whether we are conscious of it or not, we are always comparing ourselves to others. (This is why social media is so dangerous and creates so much misery).

I have briefly touched on the subject in the "Know Thyself" section in the Second Quarter, but want to get a bit more in depth here.

The people you compare yourself to are the reason why you will perfect a move and log 100 more reps—or the reason why you call it a day and watch a TV show on Netflix. They are the ones who will make you go practice on Sunday morning before attending the family lunch or stay at home and sleep in. They are the ones who will keep you on track through the lows and make to push through, or show you that it is fine to quit when it gets hard.

You can look down, you can look straight, or you can look up. The choice is yours. Many players fall into the trap of looking down when they are making progress.

When I say "looking down", I mean comparing yourself to people below you in terms of basketball level, dedication, work ethic, pre-dispositions, or talent. This will certainly make you feel good in the short term, but it will fool you and bring you closer to a feeling of grandiosity. When the time to wake up comes, it will be hard. Many players fall into this trap.

When I was growing up, there was a player from my city who was certainly one of the best around at the time. He would continuously look around himself and be very satisfied. This satisfaction made him rest instead of developing his game. Had he compared himself to other players of a higher level outside of the city, or outside of the country, he would have realized that he was missing many things in his game and, I am sure, would have worked to become a very good player down the line. His downfall was not his work ethic or his talent, but simply that he was constantly comparing himself to players of a lower level than he was.

By looking up, meaning looking at players *above* your level, you will spot your weaknesses far more easily. There will always be players to look up to. No one will ever be the best at every facet of the game. LeBron can look up to KD when it comes to scoring moves. KD can look up to Luka Doncic when it comes to passing and floor vision. If those world class players can look up to and study players better than they are, we all have plenty of options to choose from.

A friend of mine, with whom I discussed the subject of functional comparison, expressed the following well-founded critique about the concept: she said that comparing ourselves to others will bring endless dissatisfaction because there will always be people better than us.

I see a fundamental difference between the notion of comparison and the notion of judgment. The former brings objectivity and a fresh air of reality to the equation. It helps define new standards. It brings inspiration and motivation to do better and work harder on the things we want to achieve. The latter brings jealousy, discontent, despair, and the like. Judgment paralyzes action and is definitely unhealthy for the soul. **In no instance should comparison mean undermining acceptance of the self.** We must all accept our present state and play with our own cards.

I can remember a few times in my career where the people I compared myself to ended up being crucial to my development. At the age of 14, I decided to take basketball seriously. I started to train more often than the kids around me. I thought I worked hard. I would go to the gym, get my shots up in an unstructured way, and would be satisfied.

Thanks to the arrival of Coach T and my friend and teammate Paul, our U15 team qualified for the regional group, which was composed of the top six teams in the whole western region of Switzerland. Prior to that, I had never played farther than the Geneva region borders.

At the time, I was already known to be a good three-point shooter. I was definitely the best shooter on my team. It was then that I met another player my age named Simon. His team was weak, but they were competing because Simon was torturing opponents with his long-range scoring abilities. And I mean *torturing*. I can remember a game in which he buried 13 three-pointers in a victory over the top seeded team in our group. I thought this guy was from another planet and probably possessed some type of magical talent. From that day on, he became the person I compared myself to.

Due to a lucky string of events, I got to know him and learned about his training routines. I realized that what I called hard work was simply child's play for this guy. When it came to working out, he was the new reference point because he was the one person I knew at the time who worked the hardest on his game. Before long, Simon and I became training buddies. Just like that, I went from looking at the guy as a model to matching his work input.

When I got to prep school, I met Billy Baron. Billy was a good player out of Rhode Island. He was not the most talented player, nor the most physical, but his work ethic was off the charts. Seeing him redefined what I thought work ethic was.

Billy would often eat in seven minutes to cram in thirty minutes of practice during our forty five minute lunch break while we were all chatting and having a good time. During pre-season, he broke his right thumb and had a cast all the way to the mid forearm for about six weeks... He kept the exact same routine and would workout with his left hand only. No matter the time of the day, high were the chances to find Billy working on something basketball related.

I was never able to match the level of work ethic Billy put into basketball because my body would not endure this level of intensity. But throughout my career, the knowledge that Billy was somewhere continuously working, kept me motivated to do the same. Billy Baron went on to play many years in the prestigious Euroleague, and even represented Team USA at the 2017 FIBA Americup. Not bad for a 6'2" (188 cm) white guy. Want to dream? Sit comfortably, type Billy Baron on YouTube, and enjoy pure mastery.

Increasing my training regimens never stemmed from jealousy, or low satisfaction about myself. It was always about realizing that the next guy was giving more to the game I loved, and at times in a smarter way. If I wanted the results, the minimum I could do was to match it.

Always compare yourself to those above you, whether they are next to you or on another continent. Comparison, done the right way, is motivating, not deflating. It shows you new standards, new possibilities, and new ways to walk the path you want to walk.

Labor III: Work with Mother Nature

"It's not about the cards you're dealt, but how you play the hand."

—Randy Pausch

I watched him steal the ball and fly down the court at an amazing speed. No one could chase him. As he got closer to the rim, he planted his left foot on the ground and elevated. After what seemed to be an eternity in the air, he slammed the ball into the basket with such power that the ball hit the back iron and bounced all the way to the 3 point line. We were still playing in the U15 category.

In our eyes, this player was unbelievable. He was taller, stronger, and faster than any of us. Once he had the ball in his hands, he could finish at the rim. If he didn't have the ball in his hands, he could crash the offensive board and score. Pure domination. Two years later, he was nowhere to be found. He had already quit playing basketball because he realized he was not good enough. Strange, right? He was dominating the national scene as a 14-year-old and then disappeared faster than lightning in the sky.

The reason why this player was able to enjoy such domination at a young age was because he went through puberty way ahead of anyone else. He was a grown man playing with and against a bunch of kids... And he abused it—to his detriment.

As young players grow, each one undergoes their own unique development—mentally, physically, and biologically. Some enter these phases earlier, while others do so later.

Because our competition systems typically group young athletes by age or grade, it's common to observe significant biological differences among those competing in the same category. This phenomenon can greatly affect an athlete's experience, for better or worse.

Immense development advantages can be reaped by those who recognize in which category they fall into, and immense dangers lurk on those who don't. Let's look into the potential gifts and pitfalls of each situation:

Early puberty players:

These players benefit from a lot more attention early on thanks to their physical dominance. They are often the ones recruited in selections or area teams, enjoy more responsibilities, and receive more guidance and attention from their coaches (as coaches can rely on them to win). These feats can boost motivation and confidence, helping them believe in themselves and in their capabilities to develop skills and become good players.

On the other hand, those players often fail to realize that their good results are only or mostly linked with their physical upside. They rely on it to produce results and fail to develop their game in areas such as skills, techniques, and tactics. The development of a proper work ethic also often suffers along the way. Once the other players catch up physically, the party is over.

The most common basketball example of this phenomenon is players who are taller or more physical than their peers early on. Because of their size and strength (relative to their teammates who are in earlier stages of development), they play in the post both because their coach uses them to get more rebounds and score more easily, and because these players often enjoy using their upside to be prolific and get results instantly. Oftentimes, these players find themselves unable to adjust when others around them start to catch up in size and strength between the ages of 15 and 19.

Late-puberty players:

A player who grows up physically weaker due to late puberty will find and develop—if he wants it badly enough—ways to stay competitive among physically stronger players. This seemingly huge disadvantage will boost creativity, which will manifest in many forms such as specific skills, tactics, mental toughness and perseverance, work ethic, or leadership skills to name a few. These qualities are often only achievable through immense fighting and suffering—the kind of fighting and suffering that no one will purposefully go through when an easier option is available. But the payoff in the long run can be huge. Once their physical development comes up to par with the others, those players find themselves with an upside. The skill set acquired through their struggle gives them an edge—whether technical, tactical, or mental—over the others.

For those who pushed through and were able to stay in the game, the results are often mind-blowing. Sometimes, the greatest tests and roadblocks are just a way Lady Luck shows up. When there are no easy options, and the only way is to find a way, magic can happen. Sometimes, the greatest luxury to possess is no choice.

On the other hand, the disadvantages of going through late puberty are twofold. Firstly, many talented late-development players get bypassed by coaches, scouts, and selection teams, or even get cut—therefore receiving less guidance, less attention, and poorer structures for development. Secondly, and maybe the scariest of all, they often get discouraged and quit, failing to realize that their weakness is only temporary. So many great talents were lost due to discouragement.

Soccer's all-time great Lionel Messi was on the verge of being cut by Barcelona at a young age due to his small size. The Arsenal youth program dropped the ax on a young prospect who was too small. He later became Tottenham's superstar Harry Kane, one of the most physically dominating strikers in the world.

Stephen Curry, Paul George, and many other NBA players were bypassed by major universities out of high school as they were not fully developed as young eighteen-year-olds. San Antonio Spurs and Team USA member Derrick White was snubbed by *all* NCAA Division I and *all* NCAA Division II schools out of high school. He landed a last-minute Division II scholarship by pure luck as the coach of a non-scholarship college who was recruiting him, got hired at the University of Colorado, Colorado Springs (UCCS). White grew another four inches in college and became an NCAA DII All-American within two years.

Unfortunately, for each success story of players making it big despite being overlooked early on, there are hundreds and even thousands of stories of equally talented players who took a different direction due to being bypassed by all, and/ or quitting on themselves too early.

This hurdle is present across every sport.

A study done in the NHL[22] revealed that a disproportionate number of players in the league are born in the early months of the year.

In hockey, regional academies and high-quality teams recruit their players at an early age. Since categories are made by age groups, the players born in earlier months are typically more developed and therefore look better on the ice—an eight-to-ten month age gap can make a big difference. Those players get selected at the detriment of the younger, weaker ones.

As a result of being selected by high-performance youth teams, the players from the early months typically receive better teachings, benefit from better structures and more ice time, leaving the other ones with lower quality training. A gap is formed early and remains all the way to the NHL.

But an astonishing finding came out of this study. Although outnumbered, NHL players who are born in the last quarter of the year (October–December) on average score more goals and receive higher salaries than the ones born in the First Quarter. If we focus on the very top players in the league, this difference becomes even larger; late-year-born players score much more and are paid much higher salaries. These findings suggest that the ones who figure out how to gain a competitive edge early on reap the fruit of their work once they mature, and outcompete their peers.

---

[22] https://www.ncbi.nlm.nih.gov/pmc/articles/PMC5555707/

No one controls their puberty. Just because you can dominate now does not mean you will keep this advantage tomorrow. Always ask yourself if what you are doing *now* will work one or two years down the road. If the answer is no, you are heading in the wrong direction and must start working on weapons you will be able to use later down the line.

On the other hand, just because you cannot have an impact on the game now does not mean your time to shine will never come. Find strategies and develop skills and attitudes that help you stay afloat and compete against bigger opponents. Once you get up to par physically, it is those qualities that will give you an edge.

Stay in tune with your personal circumstances and work smart with Mother Nature. She has a plan for you. Once again; sometimes, the greatest luxury to possess is no choice.

Labor IV: Pay the Price

"Only those who have tasted the bitterest of the bitter can become people who stand out amongst others."

—Guanchang Xianxing

Basketball can offer so much. On top of a wide array of unforgettable moments, lifetime friendships, and exceptional emotions, it is also a vehicle to create a successful life. Unfortunately, those things do not come for free. For whatever you want in life, you must be willing to pay the price tag. Scott Adams[23] says it best: "If you want success, figure out the price, then pay it."

Here I want to highlight a few of the costs anyone will have to pay in the quest of pursuing their full basketball potential. I hope knowing what is coming will help you be prepared and recognize it as part of the process.

Emotional Pain: Heartbreak and Loneliness

There will be times when things don't work out. Losing a game, being outplayed by an opponent, getting benched by your coach despite your hard work, having bad days, being lonely thousand miles away from your friends and family, suffering injuries, realizing you are not good enough (yet)—all of these things are incredibly painful and daunting. Be prepared for them, these situations are part of a basketball life. When they arise, remind yourself that they are just temporary.

---

[23] Author of the bestseller *How to Fail at Almost Everything and Still Win Big*

Image 8: Sophomore year, Atlantic Sun Conference championship, postgame.

I remember losing the Atlantic Sun Conference championship game in 2012. After pulling two upsets in a row in the quarter and semifinals, we advanced to the championship game against Belmont University of now-famous skills coach Drew Hanlen[24] and 2017 NBA champion Ian Clark[25]. The winners would advance to the NCAA Tournament. An absolute dream. The loser's season would end on the spot. Physically exhausted from playing three games in three days on a beaten-down body, I went on to post zero points on 0-for-6 from the floor. We lost the game by double digits and Belmont cut the nets in front of our eyes. I was

---

[24] Drew Hanlen played for NCAA Division I Belmont University. He later became an NBA skills trainer and currently trains some of the best players in the NBA.

[25] Ian Clark was a standout player for Belmont University. He was undrafted, but secured an NBA contract after showcasing his skills at the 2013 NBA summer league. He spent six seasons in the NBA, and has played in China and Australia since 2019.

devastated. I wept uncontrollably and no one could talk to me for about three days. We did not just lose the game; my dream of playing in the NCAA Tournament was shattered (or so I thought).

Social Life and Other Life Pleasures

Excelling at basketball will consume a lot of your time, energy, and focus. But the rewards of those efforts, along with the journey itself, can be worth it.

If basketball is your dream, it is important to treat it as such… Stayovers, a weekend with friends, clubbing, house parties— none of those will help you get closer to that dream. When basketball training is a priority, then rest and sleep come with it. Saturday and Sunday morning practices don't go well when you go to sleep at 3 or 4 a.m. Being a good athlete requires maintaining proper life hygiene.

You may have heard coaches, parents, or friends referring to these actions as "making sacrifices." The term "sacrifice" implies that something has to vanish, die…something unpleasant has to be done. I see it as "smart investment"— putting time, energy, and effort into something that brings you joy: getting better at your sport.

Physical Pain & Injuries

Basketball is rough on the body. It is an explosive sport with heavy contact. The body is put at risk and injuries will happen.

A good way to deal with injury is to take advantage of the recovery period to hone skills in an area of the game:

- Finishes and touch with the left hand when the right hand is injured
- Form shooting if a lower body part is immobilized
- Bettering core/mobility/strength
- Visualization work

The possibilities to get better while being sidelined are endless. However, the best way to deal with injuries is to prevent them from happening. With proper load management, learning to take care of the body, and listening to its alerts, many painful and frustrating situations can be avoided. More on this in the following section.

Labor V: Manage the Mountain Trail

"The journey is the reward."

—UNKNOWN

It had been only a few weeks since I had gotten back on the court from an ongoing groin injury. For months, the days had gone by slowly, without any sense of purpose. But that day, I was back on the court. Being back, not even healthy yet but nonetheless able to play, meant the world to me.

And then it happened...

As I was battling to break the full-court press, the trap arrived. I planted my right foot in an attempt to gain control over my body. I saw my foot twisting and my ankle rolling over it. My leg—with my full body weight on it—kept sliding on the floor over my poor ankle. Turnover. I stood there, watching the fastbreak unfold.

I limped heavily to the sideline, refusing any help to walk off the court. (Before the LeBron James era, walking off the court alone and with no help was a big thing.) My ankle was screwed, but I could not feel it. The pain I felt was emotional—the worst of all the pains. I had just spent months away from my orange love, and the game was being taken away from me yet again. My heart was ripped apart. Postgame, a friend of mine came to get news of my ankle. I wept uncontrollably. "I just lost seven months of playing with my injury and as soon as I am back, this happens.... I can stop playing basketball now. It is too late. It's over."

I firmly believed that a twisted ankle, which usually keeps you away from the court for about six to eight weeks, was the dagger in my playing career. Eight more weeks without getting better and it would be too late. The dream would come to an end.

Young players everywhere have a sense of urgency about their basketball career. They put a lot of pressure on themselves to be a finished product prematurely, seeing their basketball journey as a sprint, resulting in poor management of their physical and emotional being.

I am not sure where this common belief—that one should be sprinting toward success—comes from. Is it because of the mediatization of generational talents like Kobe Bryant and Kevin Garnett making the NBA as 18-year-olds, or more recently college freshmen dominating the NCAA on their way to becoming one-and-done NBA lottery draft picks? Because players like Ricky Rubio and Luka Doncic played against men at the highest levels as 16-year-olds? Or because in the eyes of a 15- and 16-year-old, a 19-year-old is a grown man who has figured everything out for himself?

Maybe it is a combination of all of these, or maybe something different. I don't know. The truth is far from that. The biggest progress leap comes later in the basketball journey, between 21 and 27 years old.

The problem is that many either lose faith early on and quit before making their biggest jump yet or push so hard that their bodies or minds break down from exhaustion and poor management.

Stephen Curry, Ja Morant, Damian Lillard, CJ McCollum—these four guys were nowhere near any NBA scouts' lists coming out of high school as 18-years-olds. A few years later, they were respectively No. 7, 2, 6, and 10 NBA draft picks.

Along with me in the 2010 FGCU recruiting class was six-foot-seven (201 cm) freshman Chase Fieler. Chase's stock out of high school wasn't high. He had even been turned down as a walk-on by the (then mediocre) mid-major program Ohio University.[26] Just like me, he landed at Florida Gulf Coast thanks to a lucky string of events.

As a freshman in college, Chase was struggling to be impactful on the floor. He was too slow to play the wing position and too weak to play on the inside and battle down low. But he kept developing his game one step at a time throughout his four years of college and eventually became a second-team all-conference player his senior season.

Fast-forward to January 2024. He was playing in Japan, one of the highest-paid leagues in the world. Out of college, he signed a small deal in Spain's second division, and kept improving his game to climb the ladder to Europe's top leagues (Netherlands, Belgium, Greece, Germany) before making the jump in Japan's first division.

Chase was one of the rare players I've met on my journey who understood the long trail ahead. Rather than dwelling on his shortcomings, he worked steadily on his game and enjoyed each moment along the way.

The culture of "the grind" that tends to dominate the basketball world is often harmful for both your basketball and life journey. You will live with your body and with your mind for as long as you breathe. Dealing with irreversible physical issues that develop through excessive strain on the body can

---

[26] Ohio University is a mid-major NCAA Division I program that competes in the Mid-American Conference. Not to be confused with the Ohio State Buckeyes.

quickly put a stop to your playing career, on top of being be a huge mental and physical weight for whatever comes after.

The pursuit of basketball is hard and intense. But this does not mean that it should be mismanaged. Today, basketball (and youth sports in general) has become such a big business with such fierce competition that players often specialize in the sport early and train too much and too intensely, without proper load management and a mindful system to follow. Oftentimes, the body and the mind do not stand the test of time.

Many studies (and common sense) confirm it; early sport specialization is linked with higher risk of (overuse) injuries and a greater risk of burnout. Year after year, clinics around the world report higher and higher cases of injuries related to over-training.

The best athletes are the ones who take a holistic approach to training. They work on their game, but they also spend time preventing injuries through stretching, diversification of activities, proper sleep and nutrition, and learning to listen and respect their bodies through mindfulness and meditation.

Many great basketball players played multiple sports growing up, and kept practicing those sports (moderately) throughout their careers—a concept called cross-training.

Hall of Famer Steve Nash did not play organized basketball until he was in eighth grade (around thirteen years old). Before that, he excelled in soccer and hockey. Dirk Nowitzki did not pick up a basketball until he was thirteen years old. As a kid, he competed in handball and tennis. Tim Duncan was a swimmer until he started playing basketball at age fourteen. Those three players are considered among the most skilled in the history of the game. Together, they combined for five regular season

MVP titles, six NBA championship rings, and more NBA All-Star selections than I can count on my ten fingers.

It is very important to understand that good players are made over time. We often forget that the over-mediatized young superstars are only a tiny fraction of high-level basketball players. Most do not follow this fast route. Development takes time. The path looks much more like a long mountain trail than a hundred-meter sprint. There is no rush.

Having covered all the obstacles you will have to face on your journey to excellence, an interesting question arises:

Is all this pain worth it?

This question is hard to answer. For some it is; for others it isn't. Basketball is a lifestyle that isn't fit for all; it is physically and mentally tough. One must love it to have a chance to excel at it. Not everyone is made for this roller-coaster journey.

I believe that the stories lived, lessons learned, and character built while pursuing a passion, any passion, are the true reward of life. I also believe that there are few to no substitutes for the excitement, intensity, and enriching experiences truly following a passion brings. The journey is full of ambushes indeed, but it would not be special without all these risks along the way. Often, the worst moments also bring the best memories and best opportunities to grow.

I therefore think the pain is 100 percent worth it, as long as you've found what moves you.

That being said, there is no successful basketball journey without a transition into the "real world." Don't underestimate it, and constantly prepare for it.

I am of course talking about a career-related transition, with all the advice you probably hear from your parents, coaches, and teachers. Less talked about, but equally important, I am referring to a physical and mental transition in which the body is spared of lifelong pain caused by poor management.

"Winners don't quit; quitters don't win." I wrote this quote on all my basketball shoes as a teenager—the first part of the quote on the left shoe, and the second part on the right one. No matter how tough the times got, it reminded me to keep the dream alive and stay in the game.

Winners don't quit. Independent of the outcome, a winner is a winner is a winner is a winner!

On a more practical level, mindfulness is probably the most useful practice to help one deal with the inevitable highs and lows of this journey...of any journey. Most NBA players take part in some sort of mindfulness practice to manage the thoughts and emotions that come with their job as well as to keep improving their game. If the best do it, it is because it works.

We have worked with a professional meditation teacher to create guided visualizations and meditations specifically for basketball players. You can access them directly at **www.strideyourpassion.com/services** to start your journey into visualization training and mindfulness.

With the closing of this Third Quarter, you are equipped with all the knowledge you need to fulfill your potential as a player. It is now time to put it all in a system to raise your game, *and life.*

Quarter Summary:

During this chapter, we went through the five most common pitfalls and dangers anyone pursuing the basketball dream will typically have to face and overcome. This knowledge will help you be prepared, recognize situations, and handle them.

Labor I: **Overcome the Current**

A sports career requires participants to start much earlier and with much more determination than most other careers. Understand that to go down this special path, special actions must be undertaken early. Given our propensity to be influenced by our surroundings, this task is easier said than done.

Labor II: **Compare Functionally**

Comparison is inevitable. Learn how to use it in a way that benefits you and makes you better. Compare yourself to those who play better, who work harder or smarter, and who give themselves the chance to be great.

Labor III: **Work with Mother Nature**

Be fully tuned in to your personal situation. Some players develop early, others later in life. If you are ahead physically, do not solely rely on your physical dominance and develop the skills you will need in the future. If you are a late developer, you must recognize that it won't last forever. Stay motivated and do your best to find strategies to compete in an unfair world. It is these strategies that will give you an edge down the line.

Labor IV: **Pay the Price**

No matter how good you are at navigating the waters, storms are never easy to handle. You will get sidelined, you will get benched, you will have bad games, you will get injured, you will feel lonely or heartbroken... and much more. Just know it is coming. Don't quit when facing rough times. Similarly, don't get complacent when enjoying good times.

Labor V: **Manage the Mountain Trail**

The path of an elite sportsman or sportswoman resembles a long mountain trail rather than a hundred-meter sprint. If you want to become a great player, and maximize your basketball potential, the most important thing is to stay in the game for the long haul. Great players are made over time.

Keep in mind that the single most useful way to face both good and bad times and stay grounded is to practice mindfulness. We have done extensive work to create guided meditations and visualizations and help you start your mindfulness journey. Find them directly on **www.strideyourpassion.com/services.**

Fourth Quarter:

EXECUTE AND WIN

"Either change your goals to meet your behavior, or change your behavior to meet your goals."

—Unknown

In the First Quarter, we looked at seven principles that are of high importance to understand and adopt in your mindset as a basketball player pushing to reach your full potential. In the Second Quarter, we established the foundations of the MyStride Approach by defining and understanding the three pillars that constitute it and the byproduct they create. We then took a small detour to explore the different obstacles that can take any player off route, how to anticipate them and how to overcome them.

Here we are finally. The Fourth Quarter, the money time—where reputations are made. Sharpen your focus. What we will implement together in this quarter has the potential to change your life. Together, we will connect the dots and put all the knowledge we covered in a Training Management System that will transcend the way you approach the game and help you in your quest to become the best version of yourself. If implemented the right way, it will provide increased discipline, increased consistency and give you a clear structure and direction to follow during everyday training and competition. With it, you will win the day, day after day, by constantly taking meaningful strides toward your desired journey.

No matter your background or personal situation, you can benefit from using the MyStride Approach. It is fully adaptable to any player, and as an extension, to any activity outside basketball. Learn it, implement it, and benefit from it for a lifetime.

It will take seven easy steps to understand, build and start implementing your tailored MyStride Approach system. These steps will flow with the following logic. In Step 1, we will dig deep into your game with the help of a SWOT analysis to thoroughly understand yourself as a basketball player. With the findings from the SWOT analysis, we will move to Step 2 and define a crystal-clear vision, according to your given profile. We will then proceed to Step 3, during which we will pinpoint the specific priorities to work on to move towards your vision.

Steps 4, 5, and 6 will focus on the construction of your Training Management System. Step 4 will explain the notions of Daily and Weekly Strides. In step 5, we will explore how to structure the system in three layers. In Step 6, we will put it all together and learn how to include these three layers within the Daily and Weekly Strides and how to practically implement it. Finally, step 7 will explain how to keep your system up to date as you progress.

For this implementation to have the biggest impact, I highly encourage you to download the workbook at www. strideyourpassion.com/services. The workbook will allow you to complete all the exercises in a space dedicated for it, and access a 8-week blank system for your own implementation.

Without further ado, let's jump in!

Step 1: SWOT

"It does not matter how many resources you have. If you don't know how to use them, it will never be enough."

—UNKNOWN

No matter the task at hand, to move from a present state to a desired outcome, there is no choice but to follow a strategy. Most basketball players choose the "no strategy" strategy when approaching their training and workouts. They simply go through the motion. This inevitably yields random (and often poor) results.

Just like a farmer wanting to produce potatoes needs to know about his land, the type of soil, the region's climate, and any other variable that can influence his crops before getting to work, a ball player needs to be aware of his resources to have a chance to craft a sensible strategy and implement it successfully (*know thyself, know the enemy…remember?*).

To acquire this level of self-knowledge, we will use a SWOT analysis. Famous NBA skills trainer and old college rival of mine Drew Hanlen from Pure Sweat Basketball was the first person I heard of using this type of analysis to profile players. He currently works with multiple NBA players, including Bradley Beal, Jayson Tatum, Jordan Clarkson, Joel Embiid, and others.

SWOT stands for *Strengths, Weaknesses, Opportunities, Threats.* The aim of the SWOT is to look at yourself, identify the characteristics of your game, and understand your profile as a basketball player to then take the appropriate measures moving forward.

Instead of engaging in explanations and theory, I would like to work directly with you in building your own SWOT. Turn off your phone, concentrate, and take a moment to deep-dive into your game. Try to be as objective as possible as you answer the questions and go through the steps. The more objective you are, the more accurate your player profile will be. It is important that this step is done rigorously as it will be the basis of everything that follows.

Image 9: Sophomore year, Atlantic Sun Conference championship, guarding Belmont's guard Drew Hanlen.

WORKBOOK EXERCISE II – SWOT ANALYSIS

(find the entire workbook to download on www.strideyourpassion.com/services

The first two items of the SWOT analysis, *strengths and weaknesses*, live in the present. They capture who you are as a player today. They are a snapshot of you right now, without considering the future.

S (STRENGTHS):

- In what situations are you the most valuable to the team?

- What does your coach use you for at the moment?

- What does your coach sub you in for?

- What can you rely on right now to make a difference on the court?

If your coach puts you on defense against the top player from the other team, your strengths are probably your physical attributes, anticipation, aggressiveness, or intensity. If you are used by your coach to come off screens to knock down shots, your strength is probably your ability to shoot the ball with accuracy—your touch.

Strengths can also be intangible. One of my strengths when I was playing was my ability to pay close attention to details. If the coach indicated a place on the court I should be in to receive the ball, or an angle at which I should set a screen, I'd execute. Some players bring a lot of energy. Some are really positive people and great teammates. Everyone has their own strengths.

Your coach subs you in when he needs

What are your best traits as a basketball player right now?

My strengths are:

1.

2.

3.

W (WEAKNESSES):

- What are the things you cannot count on right now?

- Why does your coach sub you out?

- What are the current gaps in your game?

Everyone has weaknesses. If you cannot see any, then your weakness is probably your inability to see things objectively. As I mentioned in the strength section, it is important to identify both tangibles and intangibles, because being a good basketball player is much more than just ball handling and shooting.

It is sometimes harder to pinpoint weaknesses than strengths, here is a list of common weaknesses players tend to have. This list may help you identify yours:

Tangible:

- Weak left or right hand

- Lack of reliable moves

- Not understanding how to change rhythm

- Lack of consistency in shooting

- Poor fundamentals

- Poor box-out habits

Intangible:

- Hot temper

- Floor vision

- Focus at practice

- Communication

- Space awareness
- Work ethic
- Unable to remember plays

What are the things you cannot rely on right now?

....

What does your coach ask you to limit on the court?

....

My weaknesses are

1. ....

2. ....

3. ....

The next two items, *opportunities* and *threats*, are a bit trickier to understand, but are crucial to identify as they will be key for the next steps.

When a SWOT analysis is done in a business setting, opportunities and threats are defined as external factors, such as growing trends in the industry or a new technology or new regulations that could help or hurt the business.

Within the MyStride Approach, we will define them as **potentials**. Potentials live in the future, and will only get actualized if certain actions are taken over time.

Opportunities and threats are sometimes hard to see, because they are not felt in the present. They are only projections of a possible you.

They can, but don't have to be, closely linked to your current strengths or weaknesses: the strength of a player can be his ability to rebound the ball because he is more athletic than his peers, and a threat can be his lack of box-out and contact in rebounding. What makes him valuable to his team today will disappear and become a weakness at the next level if the threat is not addressed in a timely manner.

Similarly, a weakness can be linked to an opportunity: a player's weakness can be his jump shot, but the same player can have good mechanics and good hands. An opportunity will be the potential to become a good shooter. By working the right way on his shot, he will be able to make progress fast, as he already holds the right cards in his hands. His current weakness could turn into a strength in the future.

O (OPPORTUNITIES):

- Given your attributes, what can become your greatest strength in the future?

- What can you leverage?

- In what areas of the game can you make a big leap, if you focus on it?

Think of opportunities as the areas of the game where you have unexploited advantages that could be developed to become strengths in the future. If you have good touch and soft hands around the basket, see this as an opportunity to become a prolific scorer. If you are tall and mobile, see this as an opportunity to become a match-up problem and a great defender. If you are a physical and explosive player, you probably have the opportunity to become an excellent rebounder for your size.

Opportunities live in the future. It is a potential, but not yet a reality. It will be your job to make it so.

What can become your greatest strength in two years' time?

....

What can you take advantage of and turn into a valuable asset for your game?

....

My opportunities are:

1. ....

2. ....

3. ....

T (THREATS):

- What will hurt you in the future if you keep things the way they are?

- What are you relying on that will not work at the next level?

- What does your coach criticize you for?

Global warming is a threat. For the most part, we don't feel the effects of it on a daily basis and keep living as if nothing is happening (depending on what region of the world you live in). However, unless drastic changes are made right now in our lifestyles and everyday consumption habits, we will be greatly affected down the road and it will be too late to reverse things (if it's not already the case). Everyone knows this, but it seems so hard to take the appropriate drastic actions because we prefer to stay within our current comfort and habits rather than making the necessary changes.

I used this climate change analogy to show you how hard it is to work on something that does not have immediate effect and how hard it is to move away from things that currently provide gratification.

Identifying threats is essential for your development. It is easy to rely on things that produce instant results, but those things are often a double-edged sword. We rely on them, thinking it will work forever, and fail to realize that these advantages won't last. Here lies the root cause of the downfall of many really good young players. They could not identify the threats lurking up on them until it was too late, as explained in Labor III from the Third Quarter.

Will your body frame be adequate for your position in two years? In four years? If not, you are in danger; you must start developing skills that will suit your situation in the future.

What will hurt you in the future if you keep things the way they are?

What are you relying on right now that will not work at the next level?

....

My threats are:

1. ....

2. ....

3. ....

On the next page is a SWOT analysis example from an imaginary player to show you how to set yours up.

STRENGTHS **Timing (rebounds, blocks):** *Always catches the ball at its highest point* **Athletic abilities:** *good size, explosive athlete, good verticality*	**OPPORTUNITIES** **Can develop into offensive threat:** *Good touch and good hands around basket, mixed with athletic abilities* **Good mobility, can transition into a small forward:** *Explosive and mobile with good coordination*
WEAKNESSES **Fundamentals and basketball movements:** *Lacking fundamentals in passing and dribbling* **Lack of reliable moves:** *Unable to take defenders 1 v. 1* **Ball Handling/ball control:** *Uncomfortable with ball in hand*	**THREATS** **Movement away from the ball:** *Only plays with ball in hand, does not understand off-ball movements, (seals, cuts, positioning)* **Relies on physical dominance:** *No box-outs, small size for current position* **Overall technique and fundamentals:** *Won't be able to perform at next level unless skills and fundamentals improve*

Report your findings to get a clear and concise picture of yourself.

<table>
<tr><td>STRENGTHS

1. ....

2. ....

3. ....</td><td>OPPORTUNITIES

1. ....

2. ....

3. ....</td></tr>
<tr><td>WEAKNESSES

1. ....

2. ....

3. ....</td><td>THREATS

1. ....

2. ....

3. ....</td></tr>
</table>

Great job on building your first SWOT analysis. But don't leave it here. Chances are that your first shot was not perfect. Allow me to give you a few tips to go more in depth. The more accurate your SWOT, the better the strategy and system you will create for yourself.

JUDGE YOURSELF TO STANDARDS THAT MATCH YOUR LEVEL AND AMBITIONS. You may spot only strengths and look good compared to a player who does not really care about basketball, but this will not help you advance. Focus on comparing yourself and your game to those slightly ahead of you, and those who have ambitions similar to yours.

USE VIDEO ANALYSIS. Men lie; women lie; film doesn't. Watch your film. Don't rely on what you think you do or think you know. Missed box-outs, a cross-over not as efficient as you thought, floor vision less sharp than in your mind—watching film can hurt because the truth hurts. But it is a necessary step.

ASK YOUR COACH OR AN OG FOR FEEDBACK. Ask people in a position of knowledge. They have many years of basketball experience. They will give you great feedback.

WORK WITH A SPECIALIST. Invest in yourself. It will be worth it. We help players looking for professional support through consultancy and mentorship programs. Visit **www.strideyourpassion.com/services** for more information.

Step 2: Crystal-Clear Vision

"A vision is not just a picture of what could be; it is an appeal to our better selves, a call to become something more."

—Rosabeth Moss Kanter

Once your SWOT is comprehensive and complete, it is time to extract a vision from it. When talking about a vision, I am referring to a potential version of yourself—the best possible one—as a basketball player in the future. In other words, you can think of it as your own future best case scenario scouting report[27].

Unfortunately, one cannot simply make up any vision and pray for it to actualize. A properly defined vision should:

Be aligned with a realistic future version of yourself. Stay rooted in what you learned in your SWOT analysis. The goal is to play your best hand based on the cards you were dealt.

Be clear and straightforward. Only four sentences suffice. If you need more, you are being too vague and unassertive. Focus on the essential.

Be internally focused. Your vision should be devoid of any outcome, circumstances, or dream. *Becoming a great catch & shoot player is a vision. Playing shooting guard in a professional team is an outcome.*

---

[27] A scouting report describes a player with high accuracy to prepare to play against him, or make the wisest recruiting decision.

Be ambitious. Famous entrepreneur Vishen Lakhiani[28] states that we often overestimate what is possible to accomplish in one year, but vastly underestimate what is possible in three. Dare to dream big. With consistency over time, much can be achieved. Don't think further than three years. You will lose connection to your vision if it is too far away. I advise to think 18 to 24 months into the future.

Coming back to the player we used as an example in the SWOT, here is what his crystal-clear vision would look like:

- **Explosive wing player, dangerous attacking the rim off 1 to 3 dribbles and strong rim finisher.**
- **Knows how to position himself and play away from the ball.**
- **Good catch & shoot player from the perimeter with his feet set.**
- **High-level rebounder for his position.**

Your vision will become your direction, your North Pole star. Knowing the end will allow you to approach each training with clarity, focus, and drive. Once a clear vision has been established, every action performed and every training session can and should be done with purpose; inching you toward the best possible basketball version of yourself.

---

[28] Vishen Lakiani is the author of the New York Times bestseller The Code of the Extraordinary Mind and the founder of the company Mindvalley.

WORKBOOK EXERCISE III – DEFINE YOUR CRYSTAL-CLEAR VISION

My vision (four sentences):

....

....

....

....

Step 3: Priorities of Work

*"It's not the daily increase but daily decrease.
Hack away at the unessential."*

—Bruce Lee

In this step, we will extract from your vision what is essential to work on to actualize yourself. Here is where reverse engineering begins. Starting with the end in mind (your vision), and knowing where you stand today (your SWOT), answering a simple question will help you define these priorities:

Knowing my vision, what essential parts of the game should I work on to get there?

Pay close attention to your opportunities and threats. Opportunities represent the areas of the game that correspond to your profile as a player. They define possible future strengths. Unattended opportunities will prevent you from actualizing your potential. On the other hand, threats will jeopardize your game in the future if neglected. Your current threats are your future weaknesses. They may not be apparent against your current competition however they will get exposed at the next level.

The Pareto Principle

Also known as the 80/20 rule, the Pareto Principle states that roughly 80% of consequences come from 20% of causes, and vice-versa[29]. Translated into basketball terms, it means that 20% of the work a player puts in will produce 80% of his progress (or results). Inversely, the remaining 80% of work yields a mere 20% of results.

I am not presenting you this principle as a cheat code to help you cut training hours. In sport, the hours will have to be invested. However, if not invested the smart way, they will produce very few results and there will never be enough time to actualize your vision.

It is of utmost importance to define the few essential priorities of work that, if focused on, will lead you to your vision (or at least 80% of it). Ideally, you should have no more than three to four priorities of work on your list. If you prioritize everything, you will prioritize nothing.

To stay consistent, I will use the same player as I did in steps 1 and 2 to offer a practical example. His priorities of work would be:

- **Improve direct drives and finishes**
- **Improve off-ball movements—cutting and positioning**
- **Work on catch & shoot situations**
- **Improve box-out habits**

Notice that this player will not need to develop pick-and-roll knowledge, nor shooting coming out of screens or off the dribble in the immediate future. This type of work would be unessential and counterproductive to his development.

---

[29] https://en.wikipedia.org/wiki/Pareto_principle

Once you define your priorities of work, it could shock you to realize that the way you trained up until now was not helping your game and you may have to readjust the route to start focusing on what is essential. The impactful and necessary work may not be attractive nor pleasant. It takes time, dedication, and a lot of (smart) repetition to acquire great skills. Acting today on the things that will make you better 6, 12, or 24 months down the road requires much discipline.

Steph Curry did exactly this at 16 years old when he realized he needed a higher shot release. Tiger Woods did it after being the No. 1 golfer in the world when realizing his swing was not perfect. Are you willing to put in this kind of effort?

Retin Obasohan was my teammate and roommate for one year in college during my quick and unsuccessful fifth year of college in the SEC Conference at The University of Alabama[30]. Despite not being tall (6'2" – 188cm), he was one of the most physically dominant players I have ever seen. However, he was not very agile with his hands. His shooting was a big threat to his game as a combo guard (a mix between point guard and shooting guard).

During the entire year, he spent at least two hours working on his shot each night, on top of demanding team training during the day. His shot remained poor and unreliable. It was not until his senior year, after years of insane work and repetition, that his shot finally got good enough to impact his game. He went from averaging 6.1 points per game during his

---

[30] Because of my chronic knee pain, I redshirted my senior season at Division II Chaminade University (I stopped playing after 5 games), leaving me one more year of NCAA eligibility. I chose The University of Alabama over many other programs. Things did not go smoothly and I never suited up for the Crimson Tide.

junior year, to 17.5 points per game the following year. During his senior campaign, he dropped 35 points on LSU phenom and future #1 draft pick Ben Simmons, and was selected to the All-SEC First-Team (the most competitive league in the NCAA). Shooting was the 20% that brought him from being a poor offensive player to becoming virtually unstoppable. He is now playing at the highest levels in Europe and representing his country in international competitions.

Sometimes fixing a threat means developing a specific skill. My threat was that I was nowhere near physical enough to play at the next level. There was not much I could do about my small frame and lack of athletic ability. How did I overcome it? By becoming the best shooter my coaches had ever seen.

So, as a general rule, if your threats are a lack of specific skills, work hard at those skills until they become strengths. If they are something you cannot change, figure out how to be excellent at other things to make up for it.

Some players will need to develop their overall game and become well rounded to reach the highest levels. Others will need to focus on one or two aspects and become specialists to get to the top. Again, there is no general formula. How to work and what to work on will be determined by each player's personal situation.

Last word of advice. It is not because some areas of the game lie in your opportunity quadrant that things will come easy. There are many more players who waste their potential than players who fulfill it. No matter what priorities you set, effort must come into the picture. Remember the equation from the second principle in the First Quarter:

Talent × Effort = Skill

Skill × Effort = Achievement

No effort, no achievement.

WORKBOOK EXERCISE IV – PRIORITIES OF WORK

Knowing my vision, what essential parts of the game should I work on to get there?

My priorities of work are:

....

....

....

....

Great job. You have done all the necessary background work. The next steps will be the explanation, construction, and implementation of your fully individualized MyStride Training Management System.

Step 4: Your Training Management System

"Vision without action is merely a dream.
Action without vision just passes time.
Vision with action can change the world."

—JOEL A. BARKER

All the knowledge you acquired about yourself in the previous steps is precious and invaluable. However, unless applied with consistency over time, it will not be of much use. We will now translate this knowledge into action and build together a comprehensive Training Management System. It will feature two parts that will work in tandem: *the Daily Stride, and the Weekly Stride.*

The Daily Stride:

"We are what we repeatedly do.
Excellence, then, is not an act, but a habit."

—ARISTOTLE

Just like its name indicates, you will use the Daily Stride each day. It will help you take advantage of each team practice by directing your focus, and each individual practice by providing you structure and direction.

When your practice ends, or at the end of your day, you will take three to five minutes to reflect on the strides accomplished and input them in your Daily Stride. As the week advances, you will be able to monitor your sessions, and set focus on specific priorities for the next practices.

The Weekly Stride:

"Rowing harder does not help if the boat is headed in the wrong direction."

–Kenichi Ohmae

The Weekly Stride will give you a bird's-eye view on your progress, and help you manage yourself in a sensible way.

Every Sunday, you will devote 10 to 15 minutes of reflection on your week. This habit will allow you to take a step back and consciously be aware of the productivity—or unproductivity—over the past seven days and decide on specific things to keep, add, modify, or take away. It is an incredibly powerful tool to make sure you keep a steady path and never get too far off target. After going through your Weekly Stride, you will be able to start the new week with a clear mind and clear purpose. Keeping focus and discipline over seven days and repeating it over and over is much easier than staying disciplined over a long period of time.

Let's revisit the GPS analogy one last time to fully grasp the whole system.

When you input an address into your smartphone to get directions, your GPS works in the background; it receives data from satellites about the road situations, it calculates options, and gives you a proposed best route to follow to get to your destination. The SWOT, vision, and priorities of work is that background work. It is then all about reading it properly to translate this information into a tangible path just like your smartphone translates digital codes into a blue line.

With the proper background work and translation, all that's left to do is to glance at your phone and start walking. This is how the **Daily Stride** serves you. It allows you to set and follow elaborate, predefined actions and routines, and act on them on a day-to-day basis.

After a few minutes of walking, unsure if you are still on track to reach your destination, you pull your phone out of your pocket again and check where you stand in regards to the desired destination. If you are still in the right direction, you keep going. But chances are that you have slightly deviated and need to make a small adjustment in your route. You will then analyze how to get back on track, and get going. This is the purpose of the **Weekly Stride**. It allows you to contemplate on the path accomplished in the previous seven days, and either tap yourself on the back for the good work and keep it going, or readjust the path if needed.

Once you know the city and its roads, you start to explore for shortcuts. This is what we will call **evolving** (step 7). It is like updating the software of your GPS to a new version that contains more road options in the database. Once you acquire new skills and knowledge, and understand what works for you, it will be time to evolve, updating the system accordingly.

Going through your Daily Stride every night should take no longer than three minutes. Going through your Weekly Stride at the end of the week should not take more than 10 to 15 minutes. The habit of using this system will allow you to become much more conscious of what you do, why you do it, and how you do it.

Let's now understand how these Daily and Weekly Strides are structured.

Step 5: Daily Stride & System Layers

"Unless structure follows strategy, inefficiency results."
—ALFRED D. CHANDLER JR.

Your Daily Stride can come in many forms. There is no right or wrong. Each individual is different and the important thing is to find what works for you. Right now, I will propose a way to set up your Daily (and Weekly Stride) in the most comprehensive and structured way to allow your system to be personalized and adjustable over time. Keep in mind, my aim is not to tell you what is right and what you should implement, but to allow you to design a system that is completely 100% tailor-made to your own situation and personality.

When it comes to structuring basketball training, we will distinguish three different layers for organizational and guiding purposes.

The first layer: the **CONTEXT**—in what kind of setup your practice will take place.

The second layer: the **AREAS OF FOCUS**—what aspects of the game you will focus on (closely linked to your priorities of work).

The third layer: the **KBS** (Key Basketball Strides)—the everyday steps; the stuff you will continuously track and evaluate.

A good way to understand these three layers is to think of the Contexts as separate binders; the Areas of Focus as bookmarks that subdivide and organize the material for proper organisation; and the Key Basketball Strides as the specific theory and exercises within these bookmarks. In other words, the KBS are the actual content within the binder.

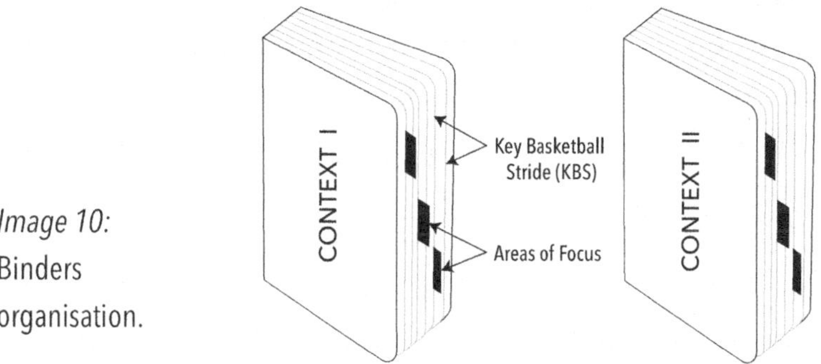

Image 10: Binders organisation.

Layer 1: Context

I distinguish two different contexts of training that any basketball player **must engage in to maximize their potential**. There is no way around it. A third context can be added to the mix, depending on your profile or situation.

1. In-Team Practice (ITP)
2. Out-of-Team Practice (OTP)
3. Athletics (ATH)

1. IN-TEAM PRACTICE (ITP). Team practice takes a big chunk of the overall practice time players have. It is important to exploit and maximize this time on the floor and get the most out of it.

When building your system under the ITP context, there are two questions we will keep in mind at all times:

- *Question 1:* What do I need to do to improve my skills, no matter what drills are being done?

Way too many players simply go through the motions during team practice drills and miss the opportunity to simultaneously develop their individual game. It is the combination of what you do and how you do it that produces results. In team practices, you don't have much choice to decide what you do (the coach does). But you can fully control how you do it.

- *Question 2:* What does my coach want and expect from me?

Remember that your coach has 12 or more players to handle during practice, and many other duties. Your job is to be in tune with his expectations and to put a conscious effort into executing them.

2. OUT-OF-TEAM PRACTICE (OTP). This context includes the training you do on your own time and before or after team practices.

Depending on school, training schedule, gym access, etc... OTP routines may vary from player to player. There is no one right way to allocate the personal skills development time. However, no one can bypass it and hope to reach his potential. Each day, a small portion of time should be dedicated to personal skills development. Nothing will happen if you simply show up at team practice and do no extras.

Training on off days, shooting sessions with a friend, 15 minutes of ball handling before team practice starts, an extra 50 or 100 repetitions of a specific type of shot each day, specific meditation or visualization sessions, or simply a few stretching sessions to help prevent injuries—these are all examples of KBS you will find under the OTP Context.

Too many players underestimate the importance of doing the work outside of team practice and fail to take it as seriously as they should. Within the OTP context, we will define what must be done to keep evolving your game on an individual standpoint.

Athletics is a fundamental area players need to work on to get to the next level. Typically, if you need or want to do some extra work athletically, you can include it within the OTP context. But if athletics is your main focus and it is a big project in itself—for example, if you need to lose weight and get back in shape or if you are coming back from an injury and need to focus on a rehab protocol—then setting up an athletic context in your system makes sense.

We will leave ATH out of the picture for the rest of the implementation and focus on the ITP and OTP Contexts. In case you want or need to include it in your system, just implement it following the same guidelines as the other two.

Layer 2: Areas of Focus

This layer is like dividers within your binder. Defining Areas of Focus (AoF) helps you stay clear, ordered, and structured. There are no rules as to what Areas of Focus to include within each context. Your AoF will be closely linked to your priorities of work. They can be broad or very precise, up to your liking.

To help you in the task of defining them, here is a non-exhaustive list of Areas of Focus that can be included both in ITP and OTP contexts. Again, it will depend on each player's situations and preferences.

- Offense
- Defense
- Personal investment (in relation to focus, intensity, and time)
- Skills development
- Attitude
- Mental game
- Shooting
- Ball handling
- Leadership
- Rebounding
- Athletics
- Recovery
- Mindfulness
- Nutrition
- ...

The purpose of this second layer, Areas of Focus, is to help you break down the big picture into smaller chunks just like you would divide any big project into sub-categories. This layer may not seem necessary, but it is very important to stay structured and organized.

Layer 3: Key Basketball Strides (KBS)

The Key Basketball Strides are the everyday actions you will take toward your passion. It is important to define them the right way, because they are your direction to follow, much like the blue line from your GPS. And unfortunately, in our days, not all roads lead to Rome.

We will have two types of KBS: quantitative KBS, and qualitative KBS.

Quantitative KBS will track an amount: the amount of reps done or the amount of time spent on a particular movement or exercise; the quantity of something. *Qualitative KBS* will essentially be a self-rating about a certain aspect of your training—the quality of something; how well something is done.

Typically, since you do not have the choice of the *what (what you do)* during team practices, the KBS within your ITP context will be qualitative.

Since you decide and have control on the *what (what you do)* AND the *how (how you do it)* outside of team practice, your OTP context will feature a mix between quantitative and qualitative KBS.

Stay locked in. If you are scratching your head right now, it will all make a lot of sense in a few minutes. I will now explain the nuts and bolts of quantitative and qualitative KBS, before showing you a template example of the three-layer system. I will then share with you a few best practices to help inspire you in your implementation.

QUANTITATIVE KBS:

As I just explained, quantitative KBS will be mostly reserved to your OTP context. They will help you **set and keep a structure** while you are training alone or with a friend, and prevent you from simply being in the gym, not knowing what you need to do and end up doing drills that do not serve you.

It is very important to set quantitative targets and requirements to your training (such as number of reps or length of time) and stay consistent with it. Without defining exactly what will be done and setting clear focus and intention, it is likely that the plan will not be executed. What we need to work on are often not the things we enjoy the most. Unless we pre-define a minimum requirement, chances are that we become complacent and push it to the next day forever. "I will work on ball handling but I will play 1v1 first...". On the opposite spectrum, the risk is to become obsessive and never satisfied, never knowing when to stop because something more can always be done. This results in over-work, constant worry, and low satisfaction.

Here are a few examples of KBS to track quantitatively:

- Number of three-point shots (taken/made)
- Number of finishes (types of lay-ups, floaters...) (taken/made)
- Number of shots off the dribble going right/left
- Number of passes with the left hand
- Number of free throws (taken/made)
- X reps of a specific exercise
- ...

If you don't want to count reps, which is highly understandable, track the number of sessions or the time allocated to a particular aspect of the game (I prefer this way):

- Time dedicated to any of the above areas during the week
- Sessions of ball handling/shooting/floaters (20 or 30 minutes = 1 session)
- Number of visualization sessions per week
- Athletics sessions: jump rope session, core strength
- Number of stretching sessions per week
- ...

Note that counting baskets made is a risk to become more focused on making them than on proper form or speed of execution to perform better in games.

QUALITATIVE KBS:

Qualitative KBS refers to monitoring *how* you do things. It is tracking the quality of the work done. These types of KBS need to be featured both in your ITP and OTP contexts.

Learning and improvement will stem from the combination of quantity and quality. Take one of the two from the equation, and the result is null.

how much you do × how you do it = results

In other words: **quantity × quality = results**

Therefore:

quantitative training × qualitative training = improvement

To track qualitatively, you must give yourself an appreciation grade. I recommend a 1–10 or a 1–5 grading scale, whichever fits you better.

For example, If you know you must box out (because you have identified it as a necessary step to improve), you can give yourself a grade on your box-out habits. After practice, you would rate your perceived performance on boxing out.

KBS: Today, I boxed out a player on each shot (1-10).

By rating yourself on the things you know you need to execute to increase your level, and constantly getting feedback in the form of a grade, your consciousness will increase over time and it will be up to you to become responsible to make those changes. The aim is not to score a 10/10 from the moment you start. The aim is to gradually score higher and stay consistent, until the habit is created or until the quality of the movement reaches high standards.

Here are a few examples of KBS to track qualitatively for the OTP context:

- Level of self-critique on each shot (1–10)
- Level of focus or intensity during practice (1–10)
- Attention to detail during reps (1–10)
- Nutrition
- Recovery & sleep

Here are a few examples of KBS to track qualitatively for the ITP context:

- Executing what the coach is asking (1–10)
- Rebounding—taking contact and boxing out on each shot (1–10)
- Fighting for loose balls (1–10)
- Communication on defense (1–10)
- Being kind to teammates when they make mistakes (1–10)
- Hard cuts to the basket (1–10)
- ...

Below, find an example of a Daily Stride. Access a blank template for your use at the end of the workbook.

Context	Area of Focus	KBS	Daily Average	SMAC Objective: *example: this week I will shoot 1'000 threes*						
				Monday	Tuesday	Wednesday	Thursday	Friday	Saturday	Sunday
OTP (Out of Team Practice)	Investment	Time								
		Focus Intensity (1/10)								
	Individual Development	Shooting Session								
		Did I comment/ self-critic on each shot? (1/10)								
		KBS 5								
ITP	Individual	Focus Intensity (1/10) (on each reps in practice – shooting games, etc…)								
	Altitude	Today I stayed calm when I made mistakes (1/10)								

Image 11: Graph example of a Daily Stride.

To help you with your implementation, I will now share with you some of the most impactful KBS to track to ensure steady improvement during your basketball journey. We will then jump to the final step of the implementation, Step 6, where we will look into the management and maintenance of the system through the relationship between the Daily and Weekly Strides.

KBS Best Practices examples

You can go from broad to very specific when defining your KBS. What is essential is to find a metric that works for you. For example, if you want to get better around the rim with floaters, you can be very broad, and commit to do three sessions of 30 minutes of floaters training each week. If you want to be more specific, you can commit to make (or take) 400 floaters per week (or per day, during vacation time), and divide it into four sessions of 100. Or, yet even more specific, you can set your aim to improve left-hand floaters and track lefties only.

The following list is non-exhaustive and I encourage you to explore and set KBS that are relevant to you personally and in line with your own vision, priorities, and needs.

Note that I will not be talking about the middle layer, the Areas of Focus, as these are pretty easy, personal, and straightforward to figure out. They simply represent general themes to focus on (offense, defense, mental, skills...).

KBS for In-Team Practice context (ITP):

As we've talked about many times now, you have personal responsibilities at practice. Your team coach is not here to hold your hand or to coach you individually. Nor is he paid for it. Your job during team practice is firstly to focus on what your coach asks, and secondly to take all possible opportunities to improve individually.

The list below offers good KBS to include in your ITP context. Notice that they are all qualitative KBS, as the only thing you control at practice is the *how*:

- Focus-intensity (1–10):

  I like the double word focus-intensity, because it regroups both concentration and effort. This KBS should be both on your ITP and OTP review until you score 8 or above each day. It is the most important metric of any practice, whether it is individual or within the team. Basketball time is basketball time. Results = what you do X how you do it. Focus-intensity is your how.

- Did I self-critique on each rep? (1–10):

  Here is a KBS to help you build one of the most valuable habits: constant self-critique. Each shot, each move, each dribble is an opportunity. Make 'em count.

  Was my footwork right? How can I make it more efficient? Was I on balance? Why or why not? Did I protect the ball the right way? Is this move realistic? Was my shooting hand too tense? Are my fingers spread the right way on the ball? Could I do this move against a good defender? How can I do this drill so it transfers to game play?

  These are all questions that you should be asking yourself as you go through drills to get the most out of them. Self-critique (positive self-critique included) is key to make small gains continuously, and compound them over time.

- Today, I [*insert what my coach wants me to execute*] (1–10):

Whatever you know your coach is looking for, formulate a KBS to remind yourself of it. Your coach decides who is on the floor. By being his best soldier, you increase your chances to enjoy more responsibilities and have more freedom.

- Today, I boxed out on every shot (1–10):

Two players can be equal in skill, size, and athleticism, but if one boxes out on every shot while the other does not, this habit makes the former far more valuable. Boxing out has nothing to do with your skills, IQ or talent. It is a simple habit that makes you a better player instantly. I recommend Including this KBS in your system and gaining this habit whether it is something your coach cares about or not.

- Today, I took every shot game-like (1–10):

Want to get better at shooting or more consistent during games? Treat every shot like it is a shot taken in a game, even during team practice shooting drills.

- Was I a fun person to play with? (1–10):

Across the world, players do not understand the value of being a good teammate. As a player, this is something I also did not understand for a long time. A player who is whining and complaining, and concentrating on negative things is easy to bench. On the other hand, a player who always stays positive, encourages their teammates, and accepts the coach's decisions will always be rewarded with more opportunities.

KBS for Out of Team Practice context (OTP):

Your OTP practices should be geared toward your development according to the priorities of work you identified. Defining the relevant KBS within the OTP context will help you structure your practices and stay focused on the essentials with continuity. Here are a few recommendations for greatest impact.

- Time:

Track the time you spend on your individual work. Record it in minutes or hours. You will quickly know if you are investing enough time in your game. Three hours of specific individual training per week (during season) is a minimum requirement for players with ambition. Three to four individual sessions of 45 to 60 minutes, 20 minutes before or after each team training, a session before school if you are an early bird... whatever fits your lifestyle; there is no right or wrong. Just be sure you track it to know how much you are investing.

- Focus-intensity (1–10):

Yes, it is the same as the ITP KBS. You want to get better, control your focus. If you are working out, checking your phone, and joking with your workout buddy, you are most probably wasting your time. Quantity (time or reps) must always be matched with quality (focus-intensity) to yield results. I advise these first two KBS to anyone starting with the MyStride Approach. They are the common denominator of any results.

- 15 or 30 minutes of *[insert specifics]*:

This can be a specific drill, a specific area of the game to work on, or simply a routine you want to establish.

- *Ball handling*
- *Floaters routine*
- *Passing drill*
- *Coordination*
- *Core strength*

- *Stretching*
- *Jump rope*
- *Meditation*
- *Visualisation routine*
- *...*

You would be amazed how good of a ball handler you can become just by seriously practicing it 15 minutes, three to four times per week. Same goes with finishes around the rim, passing accuracy, flexibility or anything else. We are all busy but dedicating 15 minutes each day in an area you need to improve is very attainable. If it isn't, simply cut down on your phone time and use it to take a stride toward your dreams.

- Did I self-critique on each rep? (1/10):

Similar KBS as the one in the ITP context. Refer to it if needed.

- Visualization/meditation /mindfulness:

We have talked about the power of visualization. Use it to complement your practices. A great start is our basketball specific meditations that you can find directly at **www.strideyourpassion.com/services.**

There is no doubt that you will quickly recognize the power of this system, and will want to charge it up with many KBS to become the best version of yourself on and off the court. However, I advise you to make gradual changes. Don't bite off more than you can chew. Start with the essential—just a few KBS per context—and build up with time.

WORKBOOK EXERCISE V – BUILDING THE DAILY STRIDE

Use the exercise below to define your Areas of Focus and KBS for both Out of Team Practice and In Team Practice contexts. You will then report your findings in your Daily Stride. Keep it simple for your first version. Define no more than two Areas of Focus and four KBS.

Out of Team Practice (OTP) Context:

What two areas of the game should you focus on during workouts?	For each AoF, create two KBS. Help yourself with the best practice list above.
AoF1 .... (recommended AoF: *Investment*)	KBS1 .... (recommended KBS: *Time*)
	KBS2 .... (recommended KBS: *Focus-Intensity*)
AoF2	KBS1 ....
	KBS2 ....

In Team Practice (ITP) Context:

What two areas of the game should you focus on during team practice? What does your coach expect from you?	For each AoF, create two KBS. Help yourself with the best practice list above.
AoF1	KBS1 .... KBS2 ....
AoF2	KBS1 .... KBS2 ....

Step 6: Weekly Stride

"Motivation gets you doing. Discipline keeps you going."

—Jim Ryan

We have covered a lot of material in this Fourth Quarter during which I have shared technical features without specific implementation guidelines. It is now time to understand how the Daily and Weekly Strides work together so you can start applying this training management system to your everyday basketball life.

The Daily and Weekly Strides complement each other. The former allows you to structure and keep a record of your workouts. The later helps you to get a clear picture of the work done throughout the week.

In Exercise V, you built your first Daily Stride by defining two AoFs and four KBS per context. Your Weekly Stride will derive from it. It will be composed of the sums and averages of your Daily Stride's KBS in addition to a set of reflection questions—plain and simple.

For your **quantitative KBS**, sum up the total number of sessions or reps done and report it to your Weekly Stride.

For your **qualitative KBS** you will calculate the weekly average by adding the grades you gave yourself, then dividing them by the total number of days you trained. *(Days without practices do not count as zeros for qualitative KBS!). See example in image 12.*

Self-Reflection

The Weekly Stride is the time to go more in-depth. During our follow-up programs, we encourage our clients to honestly write down the answers to at least two questions at the end of each week. These questions help to reflect on the past seven days' performances and reset the focus for the upcoming week. To help you out, here are a few best practices to consider for your Weekly Stride's reflection questions. Keep in mind that it is not an exhaustive list and that you can set up any question in line with your priorities:

- *How did my basketball week go?*

  This open and general question will allow you to become conscious about what you have done well, or not so well, and reinforce your ambitions.

- *What was the feedback of my coach this week?*

  I cannot stress it enough: being in tune with what your coach wants is extremely important and will help you perform better at practice.

- *How will I improve ______________________ (insert priority) this week?*

  Pick an area of focus or a KBS, and ask yourself what tweaks can be made to be even more effective. It is always good to question things to improve.

Bonus: SMAC Objectives

The reflection questions will allow you to spot the things that have not been done well, that could be done better, or that you would like to focus on the following week. My suggestion is to set one SMAC objective for the week and crush it! (SMAC objectives are my adaptation of SMART goals).

SMAC STANDS FOR:

SHORT-TERM: It is very easy to stay consistent for a week—much easier relative to a month or a year. Short weekly objectives will drastically increase your consistency.

MEASURABLE: You must be able to track it and assess at the end of the week if it was achieved or not.

ACHIEVABLE: You will not move mountains in one week. Focus on small, incremental steps. One extra shooting session, more effort on boxing out...

CONTROL: It is important to have full control over your objectives. Achieving them must depend on you only. Here are some examples of weekly objectives you have full control over:

- Special focus on one specific qualitative KBS
- Make 1,000 three-point shots
- Focus on doing what Coach asks
- Stretching routine each day
- Do a certain amount of ball handling sessions
- Go to bed at 10:30 p.m. each day
- Turn the phone off at 10 p.m. to improve sleep quality

Here are some examples of objectives that you do not have control over:

- Scoring 20 points next game. *There are too many variables that are not controllable during a game—match-ups, fouls, game strategy. Setting a scoring, assist, or rebound goal is never appropriate.*

- Playing 30 minutes next game. *Same as above; your playing time depends on your coach, fouls, opponent match-ups, etc.*
- Playing point guard at practice all week. *Ultimately, you are under the direction of your coach who has the final say.*

If you would like to add this practice to your system, simply set your SMAC objectives for the coming week after completing your Weekly Stride.

Below is the example of a Weekly Stride (based on the Daily Stride shown in the previous section) featuring the three layers of the system, the reflexion questions and the SMAC objective.

Our clients benefit from full access to the MyStride mobile app, which includes the SWOT, Vision, Priorities of Work, and Daily and Weekly Strides, with automatic calculations, as well as the weekly reflections and SMAC objectives integrated. However, keeping things on paper is a great starting point. Access paper templates in the workbook directly at **www.strideyourpassion.com/services**

Context	Area of Focus	KBS	SMAC Objective → / Weekly Average ↓	1'000 threes / Week 1	Week 2	Week 3	Week 4
OTP (Out of Team Practice)	Investment	Time		X hours			
		Focus Intensity (1/10)		X/10			
	Individual Development	Shooting Session		X			
		Did I comment/self-critic on each shot? (1/10)		X/10			
		KBS 5					
ITP	Individual	Focus Intensity (1/10) (on each reps in practice – shooting games, etc…)					
	Altitude	Today I stayed calm when I made mistakes (1/10)					
Weekly Reflection	How did my basketball week go?						
	What can I do better this week?						

Image 12: Weekly Stride example.

Step 7: Evolve:

"Evolve or dissolve...it's your decision."

—LARRY PRICE

Once you have identified your priorities, set up your Daily and Weekly Strides, and crushed your KBS day after day, and week after week, you will grow as a player. Whenever you notice a KBS becomes outdated either because you have made progress, or due to a change in circumstances (new schedule, injury, offseason, new coach), you will have to adapt your system.

When that time comes, either modify the KBS to fit your current situation or replace it with another more relevant one. You can also remove your KBS from your Daily Stride, but keep it in your Weekly Stride as a reflection question just to keep an eye on it.

Adopting the MyStride Approach will allow you to repeatedly Win the Day. Coupled with momentum and a touch from Lady Luck, I wholeheartedly believe that you can achieve success beyond your current dreams.

The ball is in your hands.

Good luck!

EXERCISE VI & VII– IMPLEMENTATION:

Find an 8-week system waiting for you at the end of the work-book (**www.strideyourpassion.com/services**), or create your own files based on the examples provided on Image 11 and Image 12 above. Fill out your Daily Stride with your contexts, AoFs, and KBS from exercise V, and fill out the Weekly Stride accordingly.

Quarter Summary:

This Fourth Quarter was intense and charged with a lot of novelty. If you have followed thoroughly, you now have all the tools necessary to implement a robust first version of your MyStride Training Management System, and to begin your journey towards increased discipline and consistency, higher consciousness, and a better training structure.

Don't expect it to be perfect from the start. It is a long process to test, fine-tune, and evolve your system. It is however essential to start somewhere. Use the seven-step implementation from this section to build your tailored MyStride Training Management System, and optimize as you go.

Step 1 – SWOT:

Conduct a thorough SWOT analysis of your game and yourself as a player.

Step 2 – Crystal-Clear Vision:

Based on your SWOT, define a crystal-clear vision of yourself as a basketball player. Think of it as a potential scouting report of yourself in 18 to 24 months.

Step 3 – Priorities of Work:

Compare your vision (possible future) to your SWOT (present state), and figure out your working priorities. *Knowing my vision, what essential parts of the game should I work on to get there?*

Step 4 – Your Training Management System:

Think of your system as your own basketball GPS. The Daily Stride will elevate your consciousness and help you take advantage of each team practice by directing your focus, and each individual session by providing you with structure and direction.

The Weekly Stride will allow you to take a step back and consciously assess the work done (or lack thereof) over the past seven days and decide on specific things to keep, add, modify, or take away.

Step 5 – Daily Stride and System Layers:

Understand the three layers to structure your training—Context, Area of Focus, KBS—and derive from your priorities of work the daily actions (KBS) that you need to continuously perform to arrive at your vision.

Step 6 – Weekly Snapshot:

Get a bird's eye view of your week by calculating the sum and averages of your Daily Stride's KBS and reporting them in your Weekly Stride. Reflect on the week with the help of a few questions, and define a well-thought SMAC objective for the upcoming week.

Step 7 – Evolve:

As you get better and circumstances change, your system will need to evolve alongside you. Update, or replace your KBS for more relevant ones as you grow over time.

Buzzer Beater:
FACE YOURSELF

"Our self-image and our habits tend to go together. Change one, and you will automatically change the other."

—Maxwell Maltz

As I got older, my interest for overall human performance and personal development grew deeper and deeper. The more I learned, the more curious I became to understand the science of achievement.

I used to believe that we engage in life activities (sport, studies, work, art...), and those who are a better fit, who possess specific qualities or talent, who work on their craft, who are smarter, who receive better education, and who benefit from some luck are the ones who achieve what they pursue.

However, after looking back at my path, as well as the path of the people surrounding me, I understood that none of the factors I just mentioned predicted success and achievement. And although these factors are preferable, success could happen even when none of them were present... or not happen when all of them were.

One day, after 29 years on this earth, I stumbled on the key. I realized that no matter the qualities one possesses, no matter the talent, no matter the luck, no matter the trainers or teachers, no matter the gene pool, no matter the work, no matter any circumstances... one will not accomplish his dreams, goals, or whatever achievement he is hoping for himself if this one simple thing is lacking:

Belief.

True, deep, belief.

Inner beliefs are not out-performable. Wherever your self-image lies, here lie your limits. The tricky part is that these deep-rooted, internal beliefs about the self and the self's relation to the world lie in the subconscious. They are very hard to access. Most of us will never become fully aware of them in a lifetime. Additionally, if we do identify them, consciously changing them through the power of thought and meditation can be very complex and challenging.

It may seem like I am slowly discrediting everything we talked about in this book. Why waste energy going through this entire process when in fact beliefs alone can drive performance? Taking a closer look into how self-image and beliefs can be created, influenced, and changed may suggest otherwise.

See, although hard to access and change via the conscious mind, self-image is actually greatly influenceable through the things we constantly do; our actions. What we do becomes how we see ourselves, what we believe in, and ultimately who we are. All it requires is to take the step of "doing" to slowly but surely create new internal beliefs, and discover a new reality.

Join a monastery for a few months to live and meditate with the monks, and you will see if your self-image changes. Quit basketball and pick up horse riding or gymnastics, and you will see the changes in the way you perceive yourself. These are drastic examples, but on a subtler level, change your approach, habits, and actions toward basketball and you will see your relationship to the game change.

The MyStride Approach will help you align your daily actions to your vision with consistency and continuity, and slowly but surely impact the way you view yourself as a player. This is where the true power of the MyStride Approach resides. It will allow you to start acting in line with your desired reality and give yourself a chance to manifest it.

I am coming purely from an implementer standpoint. I use a derivative of the MyStride Approach in all areas of my life.

During the two and a half year period spent writing this book, my self-image and beliefs changed drastically thanks to the small daily and weekly actions I set for myself. Firstly, I went from thinking that writing a book was impossible to seeing myself as an author by setting weekly writing targets. My self-image also changed by working with one client at a time teaching the MyStride Approach and getting amazing results: from not knowing how to help others with my basketball knowledge, my skills sharpened with each motivated player

I worked with, and I gained confidence in my ability to guide players successfully.

I underwent a few more of these deliberate transformations by simply following pre-defined guidelines from my Daily and Weekly Strides. I learned how to hold a handstand for up to 45 seconds and gained a new understanding of my body along the way—*by training ten minutes, three times per week over a year period.* I gained confidence in my ability to fight—*by attending Brazilian Jiu Jitsu training on a regular basis.* I changed my beliefs about my apnea capabilities and learned to hold my breath for over five minutes—*by performing breathing exercises three times per week.* Finally, I went from looking at piano players in awe, to playing some of my favorite songs and feeling like a musician—*by practicing an average of thirty minutes per day.*

Through the act of doing things with consistency, I challenged my self-image and existing beliefs and created new, more useful ones, unlocking new potentials along the way. The conclusion; control your actions to shape what will serve you most in achieving your desired destiny: your beliefs.

I don't expect you to take and swallow the words of a random 30-something guy who has yet to leave a mark on this world. This is why I want to leave you with someone else's words. On his journey to building the biggest sports empire on earth, he overcame all kinds of challenges, and in the process, revolutionized our beloved sport of basketball forever. It is Phil Knight, the founder of Nike, who in his memoir says:

"Belief is irresistible."

Face yourself; are your daily actions serving you and who you really want to be?

We have two very important and valuable sections left; Overtime, and locker Room Talk. But before moving on, I would like to ask you for a few HUGE favors. I poured my heart, soul and over one thousand days of painful (but rewarding) writing to bring *The Basketball Path* to life... If you enjoyed the book so far and got value out of it, please leave a rating AND a review wherever you got it from. Additionally, I would like to ask you to refer this book to your friends, teammates, coaches, colleagues, social media followers, and any other person who you think can benefit from it.

Reviews and word of mouth are the primary means of spreading the word about *The Basketball Path* and allow it to have the impact it is intended to have. Only you, the lecter can spread the love... If you would like to leave me a more personal note, I would be happy to read your words. Reach out directly to **basketballpath@gmail.com**. I will try my best to answer personally. I will say it again in a minute, but I say it now already. Thank You.

FIGHT THROUGH

"Life is like riding a bicycle. To keep your balance, you must keep moving."

—ALBERT EINSTEIN

Basketball never stops. But circumstances fluctuate. A lot. Injuries, bench time, bad performances, family situations, global pandemics... So many things can happen and will happen during your journey, and it is easy to lose sight of the dream along the way.

With the knowledge you gained in this book, you are well equipped to successfully go through this journey, and adapt as things change and obstacles arise. But even with the best equipment and preparation, life and basketball can sometimes seem to go in an undesired direction. This is the reason why I'd like to leave you with a section you can come back to when you go through the inevitable ups and downs life brings, and need a boost to fight through them, be inspired, and keep the dream alive. Winners don't quit; quitters don't win.

First, I will share with you several inspirational true stories of players who have walked your path and made their basketball dreams come true. Some of them you have heard of, some you surely have not, but all are enjoying or enjoyed the privilege of making a living out of basketball. As you will see, you are not the only one facing unfavorable odds to make it.

I will then share reflections and quotes I came across throughout my journey that I either collected or kept in the back of my mind. They helped me fight through tough moments. I hope these words will one day be the difference maker for you as well, and inspire you to keep pushing, increase motivation, or get back on your feet one more time (and not only post them on social media with a cool picture…).

True Stories

He was born in a refugee camp in Kenya, his family fleeing the war in South Sudan. At the age of 9 he immigrated to Australia where he discovered basketball and fell in love with the game. He sacrificed a lot to follow his passion. Let's hear one of his stories from his own words:

"There was a great training program in Melbourne called AUBD that was ran by former NBA player and NBL legends. This was where you wanted to be to improve your game. The only issue was, training started at 6:30am and we lived over an hour away.

At 15-16 years old, my friends and I used to wake up at 3:45am, get ready, eat breakfast and leave the house around 4:30am to walk to the train station 40 minutes away. The train to the city left at 5:20am. We then took a tram for a few stops, and ran to the stadium, arriving just in time to start training. Afterwards practice, we'd quickly shower, get into school uniform and make a long two hour journey back to school, often arriving late. We did this 3 times a week."

He later was able to secure a NCAA Division II scholarship at Chaminade University where he enjoyed an exemplary career, and went on to play professionally. He also had the chance to represent this country of South Soudan as the team captain at the 2023 FIBA World Cup, and the 2024 Paris Olympic games.

This is the basketball Journey of Kuany Ngor Kuany.

*S*he did not have any scholarship offers out of high school. Last minute, Florida Gulf Coast University took a chance on her. Not being good enough to play, she redshirted her first year. She worked fiercely and applied all of her coach's advice. Four years later, she emerged as the best player to ever play for the program (and remains so). She led the Green and Blue to two Atlantic-Sun Conference titles, was named conference Player of the Year two consecutive seasons and received enough awards and accolades to fill three full pages. She is the University's all-time leader in points and steals, ranks second all-time in rebounds, and is third all-time in blocked shots.

From receiving only one scholarship offer and having to redshirt her freshman year to adjust to the level, she was able to play professionally in two countries and win a championship before choosing to pursue another professional path.

This is the basketball journey of Sarah Hansen.

A former teammate of mine from Senegal once told me the story of a player with whom he underwent tests in Spain when he was around 16 years old. They were together trying to make the youth formation center of Malaga.

Prior to arriving in Spain, this player had traveled from Congo to Tanzania, and then to Yemen, following shady agents in search of a basketball future. After three days in Malaga, he got cut. Not good enough. My friend, who had been cut alongside him, explained to me how this player had no idea what was coming next for him.

He ended up finding a spot in the EBA league (Fourth Division in Spain) for barely enough money to get by. Luckily, the team was linked to a Second Division (LEB Silver) and a First Division (ACB) team.

After playing one season with the EBA league team, he moved up to the LEB Silver team. Six months later, as his performances kept getting better, he was called up to Baloncesto Fuenlabrada, the ACB team, to finish the season, where he also recorded impressive performances.

Following this rapid ascension, he was selected to represent Team World in the Nike Hoop Summit[31], where he recorded the first-ever triple-double of the event with 12 points, 11 rebounds, and 10 blocks. In 2011, he was the seventh pick in the NBA Draft.

This is the basketball journey of Bismack Biyombo.

---

[31] The Nike Hoop Summit is an event organized by Nike, during which the top young players from the USA face the top players from the rest of the world.

He was a good player in High School at Columbus East High School (Ohio, USA), but wasn't recruited at all to play basketball in college. Firstly because his main sport was American football (he was recruited to play football in college), but secondly and mostly because he played the Power Forward position at only 6'2" (188cm)...

He went on to NCAA Division III school Otterbein College, in Columbus, Ohio, where he played both football and basketball during his four years of college. And playing he did... He went on to ultra dominate in both sports, receiving Division III first team All-American recognitions in both sports. Focusing on basketball specifically, he lead the whole NCAA (division I, II and III) in rebounding for three straight season and lead his team to a Division III National Championship his senior campaign during which he averaged averaged 23.5 points, 16.3 rebounds, 3.4 assists, 2.4 blocks and 2.3 steals per game, earning him NCAA Division III player of the year.

Following his amazing athletic college career, he tried to make the NFL without success (he was told he was too short). He kept playing basketball, suiting up for the local CBA team and playing in local tournaments. With a lucky string of events and a random phone call one evening, he got the opportunity to play in for Germany's second division team TSG Ehingen during the 2004-05 season (two years after graduating from college), where he impressed. He signed with Ulm, another second division team for his second year, and lead them to a title and a promotion to Germany's top division. Ulm kept him under contract for the big jump in first division, and he went on to lead the BBL in rebounding four straight seasons, earning himself the nickname "Mr. Incredible" in Germany.

In 2010, he took a contract to play in Japan, where he enjoyed immense success, winning multiple championships and making a very good living. In 2021, he was induced into the Ohio Hall of fame. Who said 6'2" was too small to play in the post?

This is the basketball journey of Jeff Gibbs.

When I arrived at Florida Gulf Coast, there was a local Florida player who was in the grade above me. He had arrived on the team as a walk-on with an academic scholarship, as no Division I program offered him a spot out of high school.

After a decent first year, he earned an athletic scholarship, but he was still essentially a role player whom the coach did not trust very much. His sophomore year, there were games during which he did not move from the bench.

A new coaching staff got hired the following season, and they immediately saw his raw potential. Within two seasons, his stat sheet went from DNPs[32] to being the top scorer and top rebounder for our team. He was named ASUN Player of the Year, Honorable Mention All-American, and, cherry on the cake, he led his team on an historical trip to the Sweet 16, carrying us over Georgetown and San Diego State on the way.

From having no offer to play NCAA DI basketball, being a walk-on his freshman season, and recording DNPs in a small Division I school his sophomore year, he went on to get nine pre-draft NBA workouts, almost making it to the NBA. Until this day, he has been enjoying a professional basketball career around the world.

This is the basketball journey of Sherwood Brown.

---

[32] DNP is an acronym for Did Not Play

rowing up in Switzerland, if a player was even slightly talented, we would know of him. But there was this guy we had never heard of who suddenly integrated a team in the First Division at age 22. He had never even been present to a youth national team detection camp. He simply wasn't good enough growing up. But he loved the game. He worked extremely hard to get onto a first league roster and slowly earned his place on the floor. When his minutes were secured, he worked even harder. He would stay long after practice to put extra work in with great focus and determination.

He is now one of the top players in his country and the leading scorer of the national team. In 2019, he scored 29 points against Iceland in one of the most important games of Switzerland's history. He is one of the most respected professional players in the Swiss League and one of the very rare Swiss-grown players who was able to get a contract to play in a foreign league.

This is the basketball journey of Roberto Kovac.

He grew up as a high jump athlete. He was one of the best juniors in the world. But the basketball virus hit him; at 15, he fell in love with the game. Against his parents' wishes, he quit his Olympic hopeful high jump career and started to spend countless hours practicing basketball. But despite having quite some talent, he was never selected by state teams nor recognized as a good basketball player in his home country of Australia. Determined to follow his dream, he left for the US for a summer of AAU Basketball and a year of prep school.

That summer, he received lots of interest from many major NCAA schools. He chose to attend a university in the Pac-12 Conference. He was unfortunately unable to become the player he could have become due to recurring serious injuries, but he was able to stay in the game and build an amazing business around basketball after his college career, helping hundreds of Australian players with their basketball dream.

This is the basketball journey of Rhys Murphy.

She fell on her right wrist during her sophomore season in high school and broke two bones. Unable to train or play because of the cast on her shooting hand, she learned to shoot with her weak hand. After four weeks, her cast was replaced by a soft cast, and she returned to competition, shooting only with the left hand for another four weeks.

It was not until the playoffs that her soft cast was removed and she could finally shoot the ball with her strong hand. During the state championship semifinals, she shot a terrible 4-for-21 from the floor, and her team lost. Devastated, and determined to never suffer such a poor performance again, she committed to making 1,000 shots per day. She kept up this daily routine throughout her high school career (and beyond).

She never won a state championship...but she broke many scoring records, became a high school All-American, and represented USA on the junior national team at the U18 World Championship. She later chose to attend Southwest Missouri State University (over national powerhouses) and led her team to the Final Four in 2001. She also held the collegiate record for most career points (3,393) until Kelsey Plum broke it in 2017. She later played in the WNBA and earned the Rookie of the Year Award. She credits much of her success to the commitment she made as a young high school sophomore to make 1,000 shots each day.

This is the basketball journey of Jackie Stiles.

He stood at 6'0" (183 cm) and weighed 155 pounds (70 kg) during his senior year of high school. No Division I team offered more than a walk-on spot. He chose to attend Division III school Sewanee University, where he would be able to show off his skills and have an impact on the floor right away. During his sophomore year, he averaged 20.1 points per game and led his team to clinch the conference title and a trip to the DIII national tournament.

The following year, his coach got hired to the Belmont University coaching staff, one of the most if not the most elite mid-major NCAA Division I programs over the past decade. They approached him to bring him to the program, but once again...as a walk-on. He accepted the challenge, and enrolled at Belmont University. During his red-shirt season (sitting out due to NCAA transfer rules), he proved to be well-deserving of a Division I scholarship, even for one of the best teams in America, and was finally awarded a scholarship for his last two years of eligibility.

During his junior and senior seasons, he started every game for the Bruins, averaging 10.3 points, 2.1 rebounds, 2.6 assists, and 1.6 steals per game over both years, and he helped his team to a combined 51–12 record. Along the way, he received the Ohio Valley Conference Newcomer of the Year award, led his team and the whole conference in three-point field goals made as a Junior, was named MVP of the DC Paradise Jam Tournament, and received Academic All-America accolades twice.

This is the basketball journey of Luke Smith

He drew no interests from NCAA Division I schools out of high school, and went on to attend NCAA Division II program Wheeling University. He did not enter the starting 5 until the end of his freshman year, and was named in the All-Conference second team his Junior Year. He made a statement senior year, averaging 22 points and 12.6 rebounds per game, earning the MEC Conference player of the year award, leading his team to the national tournament, and becoming a DII All-American.

Undrafted, he did not quit on his NBA dreams. From 2018 to 2022, he played for the G-league team Delaware Blue Coats (and one full season in Germany's first division), receiving multiple 10-day contracts with various NBA teams, but never being able to earn a full NBA contract.

In 2022, after two consecutive 10-day contract with the Miami Heat, he signed a 3-year deal with the Miami heat, and was a key player in the historical NBA playoff run that lead the Miami Heat to the 2023 NBA Finals.

From being bypassed by all NCAA Division I programs, going through four seasons in the G-league and Europe, and trying to prove himself on six 10-day contracts, he finally found a home and a full NBA contract with the Miami Heats.

This is the basketball journey of Haywood Highsmith.

ollowing a very mediocre college career (averaging seven points per game his senior year), he spent his first year as a "pro" in the very same Luxembourg Second Division. After that, he landed a contract in Mexico for two months, before agreeing to play on the US 3x3 circuit for the sole reason that some of the workouts were run by a Chicago Bulls assistant coach.

Later that summer, encouraged by the Bulls assistant coach, he paid $175 to participate in an open G-league tryout. He made the team and became a G-league All-Star that same year playing for the Windy City Bulls. The year after that, he represented the G-league team Raptors 905 and appeared in 14 NBA games with the Toronto Raptors. He then went on to attend the Golden State Warriors training camp and made the team. A short month after the start of the season, he recorded his first career double-double in the NBA with 19 points and 10 rebounds.

He played the 2020-2021 season with the Los Angeles Lakers.

This is the basketball journey of Alfonzo McKinnie.

He was categorized as a 2-star recruit (out of 5) by ESPN out of High School, and signed to the small Division I program Furman University. After a decent freshman year, during which he averaged 6 points and 3.4 rebounds per game, he suffered an injury which sidelined him for an entire season. Following the injury, he transferred to NCAA Division II Indianapolis University, where he enjoyed good sophomore and junior years. As a senior, he exploded and averaged 20.9 points, 6.3 rebounds, and 2.5 assists.

He started his professional career in the G-League where he made a name for himself. His second year was overseas in the Israeli league. In the off-season, he signed with a team in Turkey, but after making an impression at the NBA Summer league, he opted out of his contract and signed with the Toronto Raptors. He went on to win an NBA title in 2019 alongside Kawhi Leonard. He has since then been a major player at top level Euroleague teams Valencia, Red Star and Zenit St. Petersbourg.

This is the basketball journey of Jordan Loyd.

ollowing a career in NCAA Division II at Alabama-Huntsville, he signed his first contract in Europe for a small team in the Portuguese First Division. He landed in Switzerland for year two. "I had him for pennies," his former head coach told me with pride.

After a good year and with a championship under his belt, he went on to tear up defenses in Belgium and then landed in Pallacanestro Cantu, Italian First Division, for his fourth year.

At Cantu, he gave buckets to all sorts of teams despite being only 6'1" and coming from a small Division II school in Alabama. He has been a major player in big teams in Europe ever since.

This is the basketball journey of Jamie Smith.

He rode the bench on the JV basketball team (school's second team) and did not play varsity until his senior year of high school. With no one even knowing who he was, and being recruited only by local Division III schools, he chose to attend NCAA Division III Lebanon Valley College (who?) in Pennsylvania.

He grew from 6'0" at the beginning of his senior year of high school to 6'9" by his sophomore year of college. He went on to dominate Division III basketball and was named Division III National Player of the Year twice. Thanks to his domination, he was able to get a few NBA workouts and ended up securing a spot with the Lakers in the 1999 preseason. He was the last player cut from a Lakers team featuring Kobe Bryant and Shaquille O'Neal, which went on to win the NBA championship.

He then played with the long-extinct New Mexico Slams from the also extinct IBL (International Basketball League) for as little as $200 per week and hoped to get called up in the NBA. The most he was ever able to get was a 10-day contract with the Atlanta Hawks during which he appeared in one game for less than one minute.

In 2002, he signed a contract to play in Italy's second division. This was the beginning of a 19-year overseas professional career, 12 of them spent in the top Spanish league, ACB, where he was a three-time scoring champion and was the oldest player to ever earn MVP of the league, at age 39. What a story and what a player.

This is the amazing basketball journey of Andy Panko.

He was part of the same draft class as Andy Panko, in 1999. He got drafted in the first round, pick number twenty-three, and went on to win three NBA titles. But the road was anything but smoothe.

Growing up in a bad area in the middle of gang fights in Minneapolis, he stood at 6'2" and 170 pounds during his senior year of high school. No one recruited him, leaving him no option but to attend a NCAA Division III institution, Augsburg College.

By the end of his sophomore year, he had gained five more inches and stood at 6'7". His senior year, he was not even voted as the national DIII Player of the Year (Andy Panko was). But the Lakers chose him as the 23rd pick during the draft. (He and Andy Panko were on the team until Andy was cut).

He went on to play a pivotal role with the three-peat Los Angeles Lakers and enjoyed an 11-year NBA career.

This is the basketball journey of Devean George.

She was set to play for Old Dominion University, her dream school. But something was standing in the way: They never offered her a scholarship. Being a standout player in high school, she had plenty of other options and many full scholarships were waiting on the table. She declined them all.

Despite knowing her family did not have the financial means to pay for four years of college, she enrolled at Old Dominion and joined the team as a walk-on. She was determined to prove herself and earn a scholarship; it was the only way she could stay.... She worked fiercely, and despite playing a total of only 20 minutes during her freshman campaign, her hard work and determination earned her the respect of ODU coaching staff and a full ride for the following year.

Fast forward to her senior season. She led ODU to the second seed in the Conference USA rankings, their best showing in years (season cut short due to COVID), and she received first-team all-conference accolades. She has been playing professionally in Europe the past two seasons.

This is the basketball journey of Taylor Edwards.

After being unnoticed out of high school, he attended a year of prep school at Winchendon Academy to gain some exposure. Unfortunately, he got injured and was unable to play his important prep school year, remaining unknown, and his NCAA DI dreams vanished.

He went on to accept a Division II scholarship to St. Michel's University, where he enjoyed a good collegiate career. After his senior season, he paid $500 and a round-trip ticket to Europe to attend a detection camp, where he was able to get a small professional contract in Austria.

Following his first season, he found no contract. Desperate to keep the dream alive, he decided to settle in Berlin, Germany, where he agreed to play for a Sixth Division team (a regional men's league) in exchange for a work visa and a day job. The following season, he was able to get a contract for a Third Division team (ProB), and made a name for himself. He landed a contract in Ukraine after this, France the year after, and then Israel. He has been playing professional basketball ever since.

This is the basketball journey of Mike Holton Jr.

He grew up fascinated by streetball and would spend countless hours mastering ball-handling moves and tricks. Standing at 5'7" (170 cm), he was always the smallest in size. But his heart was big. He kept working and dreaming, and always secured a spot on competitive teams growing up. He reached Switzerland's first division and enjoyed a few years of playing semi-professionally while undergoing university studies.

In 2015, with the emergence of the FIBA 3X3 competitions, his career would take a turn. 3X3 basketball's fast pace and open spaces allowed his creativity, gained through countless hours on the street courts, to flourish. Since 2016, he has been traveling the globe, competing on the FIBA 3X3 World Tour and representing his country in international tournaments. The team he founded, Lausanne 3X3, has consistently ranked among the top 12 FIBA 3X3 teams worldwide.

This is the basketball journey of Gilles Martin.

Basketball talent was not the problem. Academics were. Coming out of Santa Fe Junior College in Florida, he was ineligible to play NCAA Division I. Every program quit on him. Determined to play Division I, he drove 600 miles (965 km) from Florida to North Carolina to meet the Appalachian State University coaching staff, who were recruiting him, and figure out what needed to be done to become a Mountaineer. The answer was to attend school as a regular student and get the grades to become eligible.

With limited means, he worked a part-time job in the mornings before school, and another part-time job at nights. In between, he was found in the library working on his classes. All his sacrifices paid off, and after a year away from basketball, he was finally eligible to suit up for the Mountaineers. And suit up he did!

As the team's leading scorer, he led Appalachian State to the Southern Conference tournament championship and the NCAA Tournament. He also set a school single-season record with 103 three-pointers made.

The next summer, while swimming, he cramped up and drowned.... His legacy lives on, and a monument in his honor stands outside the Appalachian State University arena.

This is the basketball and life journey of Rufus Leach.

I would like to keep this list updated with new, inspiring stories of players beating the odds, proving people wrong, and making basketball part of their lives by never quitting on themselves. If you have lived a special journey through basketball—on or off the court—I would be delighted to read about it. Share it with me at **basketballpath@gmail.com.**

Inspirational Quotations

On keeping going and fighting through:

"The journey is the reward."
> —TAOIST SAYING, BROUGHT TO ME BY FORMER TEAMMATE,
> CHARLIE "BUCKETS" LITTLE

"Only those who have tasted the bitterest of the bitter can become people who stand out amongst others."
> —GUANCHANG XIANXING

"Tough times don't last, tough people do."
> —ROBERT H. SCHULLER

"Worry, hope, debate, exploration, error, success—this is what fills the delay between an effort to achieve something and its realization. It is the essence of being human."
> —UNKNOWN

"In order to excel at anything, there are always hurdles or challenges one must get past. It is the pain period. Those who push themselves, and are willing to face pain, exhaustion, humiliation and rejection or worse, are the ones who become champions."
> —NEIL STRAUSS

"I have not failed. I've just found 10,000 ways that won't work."
> —THOMAS EDISON

"Every search begins with beginner's luck. And every search ends with the victor being severely tested."

—PAULO COELHO, THE ALCHEMIST

"A great destiny is great slavery."

—SENECA

"Today's pain becomes tomorrow's power."

—ARUN KUMAR

On passion:

"Obsessed is the word lazy people use to describe dedication."

—UNKNOWN

"Winners never quit and quitters never win."

—VINCE LOMBARDI

"He who has a why to live for can bear almost any how."

—FRIEDRICH NIETZSCHE

"A burning passion coupled with absolute detachment is the key to all success."

—MAHATMA GANDHI

"Passion is energy. Feel the power that comes from focusing on what excites you."

—OPRAH WINFREY

On attitude, mindset, and belief:

"No random actions, none not based on underlying principles."

—MARKUS AURELIUS

"Your attitude more than your aptitude will determine your altitude—how high you go, how far you climb the ladder of success."

—GARY MACK, MIND GYM

"A bad attitude is worse than a bad swing."

—PAYNE STEWART

"Some people want it to happen, some people wish it would happen, some people make it happen."

—MICHAEL JORDAN

"Ask yourself what you want most out of life, and write down your dreams and goals. Reread your list before bed, so your mind can work on it as you sleep. Review your goals and plans regularly, until you know for sure what your life's purpose is. Then, ask yourself: Are you doing the most important things? Or are you wasting your efforts on things that don't really matter? Eliminating trivia will improve your focus and reduce procrastination."

—UNKNOWN

"You can't outperform your self-image."

—DENNIS CONNOR

"Action expresses priorities."

—MAHATMA GANDHI

"Belief is irresistible."

—PHIL KNIGHT, FOUNDER OF NIKE

"Faith and fear make poor bedfellows. Where one is found, the other cannot exist."

—NAPOLEON HILL

"Tomorrow is far, but yesterday is even further."

—TRANSLATED FROM A FRENCH RAP SONG

"Whatever you vividly imagine, ardently desire, sincerely believe and enthusiastically act upon must inevitably come to pass."

—PAUL J. MEYER

"While a positive attitude does not always work, a negative attitude almost always does."

—GARY MACK, MIND GYM

"Invest your time, don't spend it."

—UNKNOWN

"The force of his mind overcame his every impediment."

—UNKNOWN

"You can observe a lot just by watching."

—YOGI BERRA

On change:

"You can either change your goals to meet your behavior, or change your behavior to meet your goals."

—UNKNOWN

"It is only in the next stage that the actual new habit is acquired. Interestingly, if the habit is dropped, this isn't considered a failure, but rather a predictable part of the whole process of change if you don't give up trying. It is considered a part of the process of creating lasting change."

—ELIZABETH SCOTT

"Forces beyond your control can take everything you possess except one thing; your freedom to choose how you will respond to the situation."

—VIKTOR FRANKL, MAN'S SEARCH FOR MEANING

"Change is the only constant."

—HERACLITUS

On success and failure:

"I start early and I stay late, day after day, year after year. It took me 17 years and 114 days to become an overnight success."

—LIONEL MESSI

"Every failure brings with it the seed of an equivalent success."

—NAPOLEON HILL

"Success is not final, failure is not fatal; it is the courage to continue that counts."

—WINSTON CHURCHILL

"You never fail until you stop trying."

—ALBERT EINSTEIN

"Don't let success get to your head, nor failure get to your heart."

—WILL SMITH

"Learn from the past, prepare for the future, perform in the present."

—GARY MACK, MIND GYM

On being bold enough:

"They tried to grab me by the balls, but their hands weren't big enough."

—BERNIE ECCLESTONE

Locker Room Talk

Dear Hooper,

If you have read through to this point, I want to thank you deeply for your time, your attention, and your passion.

I sincerely hope these pages fulfilled the need you had for guidance, knowledge, and motivation—or simply entertainment. My aim in writing this book was to provide compact, valuable and applicable knowledge to help any real basketball lover in his or her quest to reach their hoop dreams.

The pages you just read are the result of countless and countless hours of playing, training, eating, thinking, talking, crying, and living basketball. A lover is a lover is a lover is a lover... is a lover. The seed of this book was planted in the brain of an almost eight-year-old kid back in September 1998. This kid was not supposed to become more than an average 6′1 ½″ white boy who liked basketball, who attempted dunks on his 76ers mini hoop in the guest room, turned the ball over way too much by trying to emulate Allen Iverson in youth leagues, and who would wake up at 2:00 a.m. to watch the NBA Finals every year. Instead, people woke up at 2:00 a.m. to watch *him* play on ESPN.

You most probably have never heard of me. I never made the NBA, nor was I ever close to making it. I quit my playing career early, at age 26, due to years of excruciating chronic knee pain and a few surgeries. If you see me on the sideline, or meet me on the street, you would not imagine I was ever a real hooper.

But dig a bit, and you will find stories. Stories of scoring 49 points, including 24 in the last four minutes and 25 seconds of the game in a heartbreaking loss against a regional academy (and a young Clint Capela). Stories of showing up at the right time, like the U20 Switzerland Championship Finals in 2008, scoring over 40 points as a 17-year-old and winning the title against a team in which the smallest starter was taller than our tallest starter. Stories of being the second-leading scorer of the European Championships while representing my country, despite being one of the last players selected on the roster.

More trackable are stories of scoring 31 points in one half during the 2013 Maui Invitational against nationally ranked Baylor University, which had three NBA draft picks on their roster (find it on YouTube). Stories of scoring 29 points in a game as a freshman in NCAA Division I. Stories of being third on the all-time three-point shots made record list at Florida Gulf Coast University, despite playing there only three seasons and holding the Chaminade University record for most threes made in one game (tied with my dear friend Kiran Shastri). Stories of being one point shy of the record of most points scored in a game at the legendary Maui Invitational Tournament (42 points vs. Baylor University in 2013). The record holder? NCAA legend and 2006 NCAA co-Player of the Year Adam Morrison; it took him three overtimes to score this much.

After undergoing four surgeries on both of my quadriceps tendons over a four year period between the end of my playing career in 2016 and November 2019, long gone was the thought of ever lacing my shoes again. But life decided otherwise. During the two and a half years I spent writing this book, my body started to feel better and better. I went from playing 50% defense on the professional and college players I trained, to taking part in shooting drills with them, to playing 1v1s... During summer 2021, I signed up for a few local 3X3 tournaments and really enjoyed sharing the court with my teammates and friends. In October 2021, I received a call from Team Lausanne Sport 3X3, then ranked top 10 in the world on the FIBA 3X3 circuit. Two weeks later, I was competing in a World Tour event in Mexico City against some of the best 3X3 teams in the world...

As this book is sent to the interior designer for final changes before release, I am back on the floor competing under the colors of Lausanne Sport 3X3 for the 2022 season, and was selected to be part of the 3X3 Switzerland National Team. Cherry on the cake, I am playing with more joy, more pleasure, and less pressure than I ever have.

I am not mentioning all of these feats to claim any bragging rights. My family and few of my close friends know that none of these stories were a given; for each of them, I gave to the game a part of me. I mention them only to show you that a 6'1 ½" white kid from b**f*** nowhere made it happen against all odds. And if you want it, if you really want it, I am sure basketball has stories in line for you as well.

The wheel has not been reinvented; the MyStride Approach is not ground-breaking science and the principles discussed in this book are not anything new by any means. However, applied correctly, the content discussed in this book and the training method proposed produce results—real, tangible results. Test it for yourself, and you will see.

I sincerely hope that Lady Luck put this book in your hands at the right time.

See you on the court.

Christophe.

Image 13: Celebrating the win vs. Croatia in the quarterfinals of the Europe Cup Qualifier (June 5th, 2022).

Acknowledgments

The first person I would like to thank has been mentioned in the book already. I met him while working my first job a short while after my career-ending knee injury. An adventure seeker with a deep passion for the world and for humans, he had traveled to over 150 countries by age 31 and lived through the most amazing experiences. He mentored me and taught me many things, including a life-management system which would later become the final piece of the MyStride Approach. Thank you, Stefan, for living your life with such passion and being such an inspiration to me.

This book would have never seen light without my childhood friend Joddy Appiah, who showed up at my door at the very moment I needed to seek help. He left the house as a partner of *The Basketball Path*. Thanks Joddy for believing in the project and not counting the hours spent finalizing and bringing this book to life.

To the two editors of *The Basketball Path*, Brad Wetzler in a first instance, David Aretha for the finishing touches, to the fabulous book designer Ljiljana Pavkov, thank you for being part of this blurry process.

Next on the list are all the actors who made my basketball journey so special and without whom this book would have never seen light. Some of them are mentioned in the book, but countless weren't. Special thanks to all of my former teammates, with whom I share my most profound memories, and to all of my opponents, without whom the thrill of competition wouldn't have been the same. Thanks to all my training buddies who spent countless hours in the gym shooting and playing one-on-ones with me throughout the years: Paul Costello, Simon Amunugama, and Abdoul Kachkara, in Switzerland; Billy Baron and Adam Smith Butts in Massachusetts; Charlie "Buckets" Little, Sarah Hansen, Dan Thomas, and Alex Blessing in Florida; Malte Ziegenhagen, Kuany Kuany, and Derrick Brazeil in Hawaii... And thanks to those who were always there to rebound and pass the ball for my shooting workouts, sometimes very late at night: Dan Thomas, Claudia Lopez, Leighton Chang, and many others...

Special mention to all my coaches, from the time I was a turbulent seven-year-old kid until my last playing days—still just as turbulent as a 26-year old. Thanks to all of them for coping with me and my not always appropriate outspokenness, my determination to break rules, constant aim to test the limits, and sometimes inconsiderate behavior. It all came from a deep passion and love for the game and a desire to become the best player possible.

Coaches, thanks to those of you who believed in me as a player and as a person: Coach Jaouhar, the Fiva brothers, Coach Nebojsa Lazarevic, Coach Theren Bullock, Coach Leo Gomensoro, Coach Riet Lareida, Coach Roland Lenggenhager, Coach Eric Gross, Coach Sully, Coach Ed Reiley, Coach Dave Balza, Coach Darren Wallace, Coach Batholomew, Coach Michael Fly, Coach Joey Cantens, Coach Kevin Norris, Coach Andy Enfield, Coach Eric Bovaird, Coach Darrell Matsui, late Coach

Rollie Massimino, Coach Robbie Gubitosa, Coach Petar Aleksic, and a big thanks also to the many who did not believe in me and whom I will not mention. I believe it was just about the right balance. (Sorry Coach M., I love you but you fall in this category in the way I experienced it... and I thank you for it.).

Thanks to Mark Vine, from whom I received my first and by far most useful shooting tip. From summer camp coach when I was eight years old to becoming a great friend and mentor beyond basketball, and of course, the official proof reader of *The basketball Path.*

Thanks to all the teams and programs I played for and all their staff and volunteers. Thanks to you, we could play and dream.

Thanks to all the doctors, trainers, and physios who took care of my many injuries and rehabbing. Special mention to Tannia Cotton, who cured my groin injury, to my dear friend Christopher Cornell for his dedication to get me back on the floor, his services, and the endless laughs we shared, and to Francois Fourchet, the most knowledgeable of all, for always finding time to see me.

Last but not least, special thanks to my family; to my mother who "most times" supportively let me follow my path to the fullest and was always there when things weren't working out. Nothing would have happened without her patient support. To Vivi, always cheering for what is important: following and conquering dreams. To my brother, with whom my competitive spirit flourished at the expense of quite a few fights, and to my late dad, who was so proud of his two athletic and competitive little boys.

I love you all.

Made in United States
North Haven, CT
18 May 2025